Isabella J Southern

Sonnets and Other Poems

Isabella J Southern

Sonnets and Other Poems

ISBN/EAN: 9783337006549

Printed in Europe, USA, Canada, Australia, Japan

Cover: Foto ©Thomas Meinert / pixelio.de

More available books at **www.hansebooks.com**

SONNETS
AND OTHER POEMS

BY

ISABELLA J. SOUTHERN.

LONDON:
WALTER SCOTT, 24 WARWICK LANE,
PATERNOSTER ROW.
1891.

TO

MY FATHER

THOMAS PALLISTER BARKAS.

CONTENTS.

ACTION AND RE-ACTION
OF DEATH
OF LANGUAGE
THE MINISTRATION OF NATURE
LAW
LOVE
LIBERTY
A SLEEPLESS NIGHT
THE DEVELOPMENT OF THE WEDDING RING
OF REBELLION AND SUFFERING
CORDELIA
"SING NOT SAD LAYS"
THE LIMITATION OF CHOICE
THE MARTYR
LIFE'S JUSTIFICATION
PAST AND PRESENT
THE FUTURE
OF LIFE
THE REFORMER
TRIED BY SUCCESS
THE SACRAMENT OF FAILURE
OF DUTY
THE SLEEP OF SORROW
EVOLUTION

CONTENTS.

	PAGE
Of Sympathy	26
Preparation is Inspiration	27
"What Dost Thou Know?"	28
Of True Love	29
Of Silence and Speech	30
The Joy of Production	31-32
The World Within	33
Sick unto Death	34
Of Active Resignation	35
Unconscious Influence	36
The Celibate	37
Of Maturity and Growth	38
The Spectre of Want	39
Nature	40

SONNETS OF THE CITY.

John Hancock	41
The Old Castle	42
The Cathedral	43
The Central Station	44
The Church of the Divine Unity	45
The Public Library	46
The Cemetery	47
The Rev. Frank Walters	48

Natural and Supernatural	49
Of Twilight and Melancholy	50
Is Love Eternal?	51
In Cloudland	52
A Dawning Faith	53
Praise is Blame!	54
The Transformation of Pain	55
Autumn	56
Of Children	57
Of Failure and Progress	58
Loving and Beloved	59

CONTENTS.

	PAGE
THE EARTH	60
SHAKESPEARE	61
JOHN MILTON	62
ROBERT BROWNING	63
THE RISING TIDE	64
A MAGNETIC PERSONALITY	65
THE GIFT OF HOPE	66
THE POINT OF VIEW	67
SUBTERRANEAN CURRENTS	68
TO EACH, HIS OWN	69
IS THERE ANY END?	70
"HE THAT LOVETH HIS LIFE SHALL LOSE IT"	71
OF EDUCATION BY CHOICE	72
SUFFER, AND BE STRONG	73
OF PRESENTIMENTS	74
OF EXISTENCE AND LIFE	75
IN OXFORD	76
DISUSE AND DECAY	77
LIMITED AND LIMITLESS	78
OF PASSION	79
THE NINETEENTH CENTURY	80
AFTER RAIN	81
A SELFISH PARADISE	82
DRIVEN OUT!	83
OF GENIUS AND HUMILITY	84
THE TELEGRAPH WIRES	85
THE SPRING-TIME OF LOVE	86
NEW YEAR'S EVE	87
A TRAGEDY	88
OF SEEMING WASTE	89
THE INDESTRUCTIBILITY OF HOPE	90
MATTER AND SPIRIT	91
OF HEROISM	92
HIDDEN	93
THE WAGES OF SIN	94-95
SUSPENSE	96
AMONG THE HILLS	97

CONTENTS.

	PAGE
Vicarious Suffering	98
The Discoverer	99
Carnival	100
Lent	101
Conversion	102
A Reverie	103
Of Blindness	104
The Evolution of Womanhood	105-107
A Sunbeam	108
Then and Now	109
Of Immortality	110
Of Pruning and Production	111
"The Divine Unrest"	112
Of Consciousness	113
Tears	114
Christmas Day	115
The Boiling Point	116
Repentance and Restitution	117
The Lily	118
An Open Grave	119
The Pagan's Protest	120
Expectation is Prophecy	121
A Retrospect	122
Look Upward	123
Of Sorrow	124
Of Discontent	125
A Bride's Birthday	126
"Out of the Eater cometh forth Meat"	127
The Pioneer of Progress	128
Rest, or Renewed Activity	129
Of Sincerity	130
Count Tolstoï	131
Of Gravitation	132
Of Selfishness	133
A Sensitive Plate	134
A Gospel of Science	135
The Elasticity of Time	136

MISCELLANEOUS POEMS.

	PAGE
NATURE'S MASQUERADE	137
SEARCH IS BEST	141
THE DYING BOY	143
THE HEART'S REPLY	144
THE RULING POWER	145
THE VERY GATE OF HEAVEN	148
CHANGES	149
A LIFE'S REVELATIONS	150
OF TRIFLES	154
FULFILLED, YET UNFULFILLED	155
OF CHOICE	158
THE HARVEST MOON	159
THE REALM OF MUSIC	162
MY RING	163
A DAY-DREAM	164
THE SISTERS	169
A DAY IN JUNE	171
THE PROGRESS OF LIBERTY	173
ESCAPED!	175
DREAMS	176
THE SEARCH FOR TRUTH	178-182
THE AGED FISHERWOMAN	183
AN AUTUMN MORNING	185
NOT FALLEN, BUT EVOLVING	186
TWILIGHT THOUGHTS	188
WHENCE?	191
A CHRISTMAS STORY	192
LORD ARMSTRONG	200
PICTURES OF A LIFE	202
SNOW IN SPRING	204
"OUT OF MUCH TRIBULATION"	205
THE MANY AND THE FEW	207
IN MAGDALEN CHAPEL	209
FLEETING OR IMMORTAL	211
OF BEAUTY	213

	PAGE
RE-UNION	216
CAST THY BREAD UPON THE WATERS	217
LYDIA	218
VARIETY	221
BEFORE THE CURTAIN	222
ON THE STAGE	223
A FUSION OF MIND AND MATTER	224
THROUGH BROTHER TO BROTHERHOOD	226
"ONE THING I KNOW"	230
PRESENT, THOUGH UNSEEN	231
A SUCCESSFUL MAN	233
HOPE AND RESIGNATION	235
TIMES OF TRANSITION	236
THE ALTAR LAMP	239
TRUE HAPPINESS	242
THE THIRST FOR KNOWLEDGE	243
A HARVEST VISION	245
HOME AGAIN!	247
"THOUGHTS ARE THINGS"	249
"BENEATH THE STARS"	250
THE GATE OF PEACE	253
TWIN-STARS	255
THE PURSUIT OF PLEASURE	257

PREFACE.

INTO THE OCEAN.

Upon an isle I stand,
And all around the restless ocean flows;
I hear its ceaseless surging as it goes
    Through caves along the strand;
And as I gaze, it seems that all I learn,
Or dream, or think, is like the tiny burn
    That gurgles past my feet,
    Those mighty waves to greet,
So small it is, while O, where'er I turn,
    The seething main outspreads,
    Till with the sky it weds,
Nor ends e'en there, where earth seems heaven to meet.
Despairingly my heart begins to beat,
    " Why labour so?" it asks;
    " Too arduous are the tasks
Of this great world for hands so weak as thine."

> But sunbeams glinting, fall
> Athwart the moss-grown wall,
> And on the murmuring streamlet brightly shine,
> Flashing consoling messages divine
> Into my heavy eyes;
> "Life's smallest never dies,"
> The brooklet whispers, running to the sea,
> Content to freshen that infinity!

I. J. S.

23rd March, 1891.

SONNETS AND OTHER POEMS.

ACTION AND RE-ACTION.

Upon a Mount of Vision, with clear eyes,
   One stands for whom the walls of space dissolve :
   He sees the doer and the deep resolve,
The act accomplished. Then the action flies
To set in motion force that never dies ;
   It passes worlds which round the sun revolve,
   Strange consequences in its mesh to involve,
While still in seeming death the agent lies.
Upon himself his deed must needs re-act,
   Or here or there 'twill come back to his hand ;
   And with it all the unexpected band
It brought to life. Around him then, intact
For good or ill, unbroken and compact,
   The circle of his influence shall stand !

OF DEATH.

I LAY and looked at Death. His face was mild;
   He took me in his arms to ease my pain,
As mothers lift a weary, helpless child,
   And then,—ah! then, he laid me down again,
And whispered gently as he calmly smiled,
   "'Tis yet a little while ere thou shalt gain
The Silent Land." The snowy pillows piled
   Grew wet with disappointment's bitter rain.

To almost know what lies beyond the grave,
   To be returned upon this rugged shore,
     To struggle back to health and strength once more—
May God my loved ones from such trial save!
And yet 'tis His to use the life He gave;
   His purposes no mortal may explore.

OF LANGUAGE.

IN words, as in a clinging drapery,
Men clothe an evanescent, shrinking thought,
And send it forth. By passing breezes caught
Upon its errand swiftly doth it flee
From home to home, from land to land, to be
　A guest most gladly welcomed, and full fraught
　With inspiration from its fountain brought.
It whispers hope and peace to misery,
And breathes upon a frost-bound heart to thaw
　Its icy bands, that it may run and sing,
　To other souls reviving water bring:
Then wakes a sleeping fancy to explore
A magic land it never saw before
　The world within, which there lay slumbering.

THE MINISTRATION OF NATURE.

The bud is forming long within its sheath,
   Compressed in that small space with matchless skill,
   Unnoticed by men's careless eyes, until
In some warm, genial hour, its clenchèd teeth
Spring open, that the petals furled beneath
   May spread their wings and flutter at their will,
   Their growing life with summer sunshine fill,
And weave themselves into a perfect wreath.

Then, tossed upon the zephyr's balmy breath,
   They send their perfume forth upon the air,
   Content to be so sweet, so pure, and fair,
To live retired; to welcome coming death,
   If but one heart be cheered to see them there,
   Or one sad soul be saved from dire despair.

LAW.

A LIGHTHOUSE with its clear, revolving glare,
  Shines o'er a waste of waters, while the waves
  Rush up to kiss its feet; through hollow caves
Resounding on the surf-tormented air
Their voices moan. The lifted light doth wear
  Its crown serenely; it is set too high
  To share the eager life beneath its eye.
The way it points, 'tis all it can or dare!

"Wild hearts," saith Law, "the haven lies before,
  Beware the jagged rocks strewn at my base,
  I warn you from this danger circled place,
Where grasping wreckers wait upon the shore.
Go, go from hence, be wise, return no more."
  Men go, or stay, no tears bedew her face.

LOVE.

On just and unjust, valley, plain, and hill
   Th' impartial sun looks down : strange power hath he
   To bring to birth life's hidden mystery.
He shines, and woods awake ; the mountain rill
Runs swiftly; songsters' mating raptures fill
   The forest and the field ; the restless sea
   Reflects his beams and draws breath happily;
Intuitive his gentleness and skill.

"O man," saith Love, "I make rough places plain,
   I rise, and lo! the desert brings forth flowers,
   And though in torrid hearts the reptile cowers,
Drain thou the slough and plant it well with grain,
And where miasma breathed pure joy shall reign ;
   I bring the rainbow with my sunny showers !

LIBERTY.

FAIR LIBERTY, with gentle, modest mien,
   Comes bearing lilies on her outstretched arms;
   She fears no inquisition's secret harms.
To her pure heart all men are brothers seen,
The universe to her hath ever been
   A beauteous home. Of wars' abhorred alarms
   She never hears, for her soft accent calms
The passions, as though force had never been.

She sets men free their strife-scarred souls to cure,
   Breaks all their chains, and bids them learn to move,
   Then sit at Wisdom's feet, and learn to love.
The filthy rags of Licence cease to lure
An open soul, grown healthy, strong, and pure,
   And heavenly songs are sung in every grove.

A SLEEPLESS NIGHT.

PROCESSIONS of strange faces passing by
   With smile or scowl look down, then onward glide;
The heavy wingèd moments cease to fly,
   And darkness groans and creaks beneath their stride.
To pierce the shadeless blackness wide eyes try,
   While billows of wild phantasy deride
The toiling brain, unable to apply
   A searching test of action, and divide
The seeming from the solid. Hours are years
   As dawn delays to place upon the brow
     Her cooling fingers, with their spells of light,
     So potent to disperse the taunts of night.
   Be patient; morn must break; yea, even now
Precipitates the gloom and stills thy fears.

THE DEVELOPMENT OF THE WEDDING RING.

THE world grows nobler as it grows in age!
The fetter welded on the bare left arm
Of captured maid filled her with wild alarm,
And made her shrink before her captor's rage.
But years roll on, and custom comes to assuage
   The fierceness of the bond with its sure balm;
   A golden bracelet bodes no threat'ning harm,
Becomes an honour at a later stage.

To-day a tiny circlet is enough
   To bind the willing captive to a vow
     Which she, before an altar standing, gave
To him she loved; and though her life be rough,
   No force is needed to retain her now;
     She holds her marriage sacred till the grave!

OF REBELLION AND SUFFERING.

"THE fire will burn," the tender mother saith,
   And yet the wilful child its power must try;
   Then being burnt, he crieth bitterly
Against the cruel heat with sobbing breath.
"O youth, the round of pleasure withereth
   The heart, and draineth its deep fountains dry;"
   Yet all in vain the teacher's warning cry,
For naught will stay the young save pain or death.

If children fall, the earth will never shrink,
   It keeps its place, and holds its even way,
   For cries, complaints, or tears it cannot stay.
The rebels 'gainst its laws stand on the brink
Of dire disaster, yet 'twere worse, I think,
   If for rebellion suffering did not pay.

CORDELIA.

O MIRROR of a noble womanhood,
  No fulsome syllable falls from thy lips,
  The rags of flattery thy strong heart strips
With loathing from thy speech; and thou hast stood
For duties quietly fulfilled, for good
  Unconquered and unconquerable still;
  For moral courage and a stalwart will
To do what true hearts may and honour should.

Thou seem'st at first to lack the gentleness
  Of maiden nurtured in a kingly court;
  But who may know the battles thou hadst fought
Against foul spite, masked by a smooth address!
And thou art proved by life to be no less
  Than heroine, in deed, as well as thought.

"SING NOT SAD LAYS."

Sing not O poet, sad and mournful lays,
    And thou musician, play no minor tone;
    Then bid the sea forget that she can moan,
The sun deny dark winter's coming days,
And let the morning shine without a haze,
    And happy laughter drown each long drawn groan,
    All hearts their tender memories disown,
Lest on sad sights men's eyes aghast should gaze.

It may not be! The happy need no songs;
    But while the world remains, sad eyes will stream,
    And frozen hearts will hope to catch a beam
Of human sympathy; the tried soul longs
    To know if men are callous as they seem,
Indifferent to their fellow-creature's wrongs!

THE LIMITATION OF CHOICE.

I.

THE tree knows not its office to the air,
  The stream is quite unconscious whence it flows,
  O'er shallows and o'er rugged rocks it goes
To ends unknown; and yet it does not dare
To wait until its course is clear or fair.
  Against obstructions, through ravines and woes
  Which bid it rend its locks and roar, it knows
No rest, no pause, but moves for ever, there!
And shall a few poor tears cause man to stay
  Within the narrow limits of the seen?
  Shall he remain content with what hath been,
Or follow his own tendency's strange way,
And take his share in struggles of to-day,
  His ear unto the future listening lean?

THE LIMITATION OF CHOICE.

II.

'Tis idle thus to question if man will
   Move on, as though 'twere given him to choose;
   His noblest power through sloth he needs must lose,
But no man may the gathering water still.
If he build walls, surround himself, his skill
   Must find an outlet too, and either use
   His surplus energy, or so abuse
His life, that it is tapped some slough to fill.
Ah me, I listen long at Nature's breast,
   And wish that she would cease from parables!
   There is so much her varied storehouse tells
For which man seeks with endless, anxious quest,
And yet, except to those who love her best,
   Her lips are sealed, and dry her living wells.

THE MARTYR.

THROWN to the beasts, a shameful death he dies,
 The crowning horror of a barbarous show;
Upon the ground his mangled body lies,
 While sighing night winds o'er him come and go.
Deserted he, and dead! His moans and cries
 Have pierced the pitying heavens at last, and lo!
Through darkest blue of midnight hither hies
 A shining band, to bear him from his woe.

On swift unwearied pinions he ascends
 From scenes of strife, to regions calm above.
The beauty of the crown by far transcends
 The torture of the cross; peace, like a dove,
Descends upon him, as he upward wends
 Enfolded in the radiancy of love.

LIFE'S JUSTIFICATION.

THE happy mother, with her first-born laid
   Within her arms, rejoices that it cried;
   And let the world the artist's work deride,
The scorn is naught to him, for he has paid
His debt; his thought in glowing hues arrayed
   Is born. Production only can decide
   If man, or tree, to live is justified;
For life has either blossomed or decayed.

The healthy tree must grow and bring forth fruit,
   Or generous leafy shade, for those who toil;
   Alive at every pore, 'twere hard to spoil
Its heart, for sap is springing from its root,
Is flowing freely to its farthest shoot,
   And giving strength, decay and death to foil.

PAST AND PRESENT.

The Past with fixéd features lies behind,
  No mantling blush endears her visage cold,
  Her form is cast in monumental mould,
The hands are still, the sculptured eyes are blind,
Strange hieroglyphs upon her robes I find
    And seek some clue to priceless tales, untold
    Since living youth and beauty round her rolled.
And loving hearts her secret lore divined.

Both Past and Future must abide for aye;
    The Present wanes, e'en as her name I speak,
    She waits not till I stoop to kiss her cheek,
But slips from my embrace; and where she lay,
The Past, unchangeable, mocks my lips' play
    And laughs to scorn, my cry for her I seek.

THE FUTURE.

The Future flits before me, while I race
   To catch her scented garments as she flies.
   Ah! she disdains my eager, urgent cries,
That she should slacken her aerial pace,
Permit me but one glance at her fair face.
   She flits and flits; my ardour never dies,
   "Did I possess thee, I were good and wise,"
Yet unrelentingly she veils her grace.

Shall I e'er hold that lovely flutt'ring thing
   Within my hand, and kiss her bloom away?
   Shall she elude me ever, and for aye,
While I my love-sick praises to her sing?
'Twere better so; no present hour can bring
   A gift so glorious as the Future may!

OF LIFE.

To work and sleep, to love, to think and learn!
How full is life of ever-springing joy,
Unsullied, purest gold, without alloy,
Which every heart e'en here, and now, may earn,
If but the fire of earnest effort burn
All dross away; and once for all destroy
Men's vicious pleasures: leave them free to employ
Their gifts for good. Sin's punishments are stern!
She blights the blossoms in the bud, and shakes
The unripe fruit from the impoverished tree;
She seems far gayer than calm purity,
But 'tis a painted mask which loosely quakes
Upon a grinning skull. The pure are free
To learn through countless years what life may be!

THE REFORMER.

(THREE SONNETS.)

I.

He stands proclaiming a gigantic scheme
   Of world reform; the naked shall be clad,
   The hungry fed, the darkest lives made glad;
From vice and poverty he will redeem
The thousands on whose dreary lives no gleam
   Of hope has fallen. Worldlings call him mad;
   Yet he gives up the ease he might have had,
For this divine, self-sacrificing dream.

With little help he works, yet never quails
   Before the scoffing words opponents use;
   If they their power so harmfully abuse,
'Twere worse, he thinks, to be the man who rails,
Than he who tries to do his best and fails;
   If but the conscience naught can find to accuse.

TRIED BY SUCCESS.

II.

BEYOND his wildest hope his cause succeeds,
    And autocratic grow his stern commands,
    At one shrine only men may clasp their hands;
He shows no pity for outsiders' needs,
No longer for the world his proud heart bleeds;
    He thinks but seldom of the soul's demands,
    His forces 'gainst the other sects he bands,
Defender of one more, of many creeds.

The holy fire that flamed within his breast
    Is smould'ring now beneath a load of state;
His sounding words and high uplifted crest
    Are signs ironical of ruthless fate,
Which, by success, has put him to the test;
    He loved a world, yet doth his brother hate!

THE SACRAMENT OF FAILURE.

III.

An aged man, in prison and alone,
   Reviews the past. He sees himself again
   As once he stood, a youth beneath the rain
Of ignominy borne without a moan :
And then, the tender heart became as stone,
   He sees the man inflicting the same pain
   Youth had endured, yet had endured in vain,
Since out of suffering pity had not grown !

And now, in failure's dark and searching hour,
   He sees himself as he had hoped TO BE,
   And as he IS ! O dread eternity
Of such a moment ! Shall the sad heart flower,
Or like a craven, at the crisis cower ?
   He blossoms into true humility !

OF DUTY.

Duty,—men say,—though hard, is always clear,
And he who runs may see her rugged road,
Though oft necessity alone can goad
His bleeding feet to tread the path; so sheer
It is, so difficult, so dull and drear.
   Yet many ways lead out into the dark,
   And not one steady light emits a spark
To say, "This is the way, be of good cheer."

O God, how shall men know what they should do,
   When diverse duties lie before, behind,
When rousing voices cry, "Pursue, pursue
   The stony upward track the truth to find."
And wailing words of weaklings echo through
   The keen hill air, " To leave *us* were unkind."

THE SLEEP OF SORROW.

STRANGE, undefined, unmeasured land of Sleep,
  Where facts and fancies fall in finest spray,
  Dashed from the ebbing tide of waking day;
Where past and present wondrous revels keep,
And spectral shadows of the future creep
  Behind the veil of sense, to fade away;
  Where blackest robes of grief turn neutral grey,
And swollen eyes forget awhile to weep.
The bounds of time and space are all destroyed,
  And that which is, is as it ne'er had been;
  The non-existent treads there, plainly seen.
While stripped of flesh, the spirit upward buoyed,
Trembles to find its wing beat a vast void,
  And falling,—falling,—wakes to anguish keen.

EVOLUTION.

GREAT Nature seems a Fury blind with rage,
Devoid of plan, the slave of any chance,
To those who judge her with a passing glance,
Nor ever care to scan her wondrous page.
They let the outward show their thoughts engage,
And watch the whirling dust clouds wildly dance,
But never note the long and slow advance
Through all the centuries; how stage by stage
The lower into higher forms evolve,
The monstrous to the human ever tend,
And rage declines, while reason comes to bend
The stubborn will of men, till they resolve
To leave to brutes the coarser life, and wend
Upon the path of progress to the end!

OF SYMPATHY.

The life which pulsing throbs and thrills through me
   Is as intense in you, and permeates
     The universe: all sad and happy states
Of toiling, erring, hoping men, agree
In this one thing; each in himself doth see
   The centre of the world, and watching, waits
   Coming events, as though all God creates
Were formed for his content or misery.

Could man but realise that each man's heart
   Is sensitive to sound and sight as this
Which beats in his own breast, how great a part
   Of suffering were spared, or changed to bliss,
Through gentle tones and touches, from which start
   More subtile raptures than from lover's kiss.

PREPARATION IS INSPIRATION.

INSPIRÈD men and women seem to be
  Those delicately poised and tutored minds
  The Spirit of an age most surely finds
Prepared the trend of human thought to see;
Who, from dogmatic prejudice quite free,
  Are sensitive to each fresh impulse brought
  Within the vortex of revolving thought;
Who work, they know not why, yet steadily.

These are the plates which ever ready stand,
  And only need the sun and focussed range
  To photograph the shadowy forms and strange,
Already shaping 'neath the Future's hand,
  In her dim workshops, where she doth arrange
What shall come next, in sea or air, on land.

"WHAT DOST THOU KNOW?"

What dost thou know, O sage, at thy life's close,
  Thou, who hast spent thy life in arduous quest
  Of all that knowledge yields of purest, best,
Regardless of thy private pains or woes?
What hast thou heard, O poet, list'ning long
  To Nature and the beating human heart,
  So ready to yield secrets to thy art,
And give thee ore, that thou mayst weld to song?
What have ye learned, ye gifted men and true,
  Who by so many avenues have sought
  To thread the maze of labyrinthine thought,
That feebler feet may safely follow through?
With one accord they say, "We saw a light
That fringed the garments of the Infinite."

OF TRUE LOVE.

IN that it forces men to do their best,
  True human love is like the love of God,
  And will not spare the stinging of the rod,
If that be needed, to urge on the quest
Of the divine idea dimly impressed
  Upon the inmost essence of the soul;
  And till the loved one find the glorious whole,
Pure love prevents it sinking into rest.

If then thy love bid thee with syren voice
  Content thyself among the herd to stay,
  Arouse at once, and put that love away
While there is time to make a nobler choice.
Then shall the powers of good o'er thee rejoice,
  And cry from star to star, "He will obey."

OF SILENCE AND SPEECH.

Silence—'tis said—is golden! yet it seems
  To some the parchèd gold of desert sands,
    Dreary and desolate, where mirage stands
Luring the thirsty traveller, who deems
That he shall drink, for he afar caught gleams
  As of a shining lake beneath the sun,
    Yet sadly is deceived, for he hath won
But phantoms bodiless as are his dreams.

Ah, when an eager, longing, lonely soul
  Athirst for sympathy, companionship,
    Meets Silence, 'tis more cruel than the grave!
But Speech, like summer thunder's passing roll,
  Relieves the air and cools the fevered lip,
    While its soft showers the drooping flowers lave.

THE JOY OF PRODUCTION.

I.

DOTH earth delight to clothe herself in green,
   And is the quiv'ring of the summer flowers
   The artist's rapture, as his growing powers
Evolve the image which his soul hath seen?
Do birds their thrilling inspiration glean
   From sky or sea, from air, or earth's fair bowers,
   And are they sad when angry Nature lowers
With frowning brow, to dull their lustrous sheen?

I know not. Nature keeps her secrets well,
   But man with his mysterious gift of speech,
   Inspired himself, his fellow-men can teach;
And diving deeply, wondrous tales can tell
Of those strange yearnings no success can quell,
   Of fairest forms that flit beyond his reach.

THE JOY OF PRODUCTION.

II.

O HAPPY children, unto whom 'tis given
    Fair dreams to shape with chisel, pen, or brush!
    E'en thunderbolts are powerless to crush
The man who knows why gloomy skies are riven;
To pierce the storm-cloud's secret he has striven,
    To understand life's ripples and its rush,
    The human heart, the rose's beauteous blush,
And how the soul from all its past is shriven.

Exhilarating 'tis the pen to poise,
    And linger just a moment—then begin
    A harvest of ungarnered thought to win,
Or break within a prism that destroys
    Invisibility, the common air,
    Till common things celestial colours wear.

THE WORLD WITHIN.

A WORLD within a world are such as we,
  With regions frozen fast and icy cold;
And torrid zones of wildest phantasy,
  Where unguessed possibilities unfold
Beneath the noonday sun's intensity;
  And unexplorèd continents, where gold
Lies massed in virgin richness, though none see
  The hidden treasure. Would that men were bold
To search themselves and say what there they find,
  Undaunted by the forests dark and dense,
The undergrowth entangled of the mind;
  Then seek the springs of thought, and learn from
    whence
The aspirations and the passions wind
  Into the trodden realm of sight and sense.

SICK UNTO DEATH.

THE blinds are drawn, shut out the garish day,
  Upon its couch a failing body lies,
  While hour by hour its power of living dies;
Attenuate through gradual decay,
'Tis falling fast from healing force away.
  A slower, smaller stream its need supplies,
  Till life lays down its sceptre with deep sighs
And on the face falls pallor, ashen grey.
Ah, shall a soul wound-weakened to its core
  By long intrusion of unholy life,
  Or by neglect's two-edged, remorseless knife
Waste all its essence on the earth's mud floor,
  Grow weaker and yet weaker till all strife
Is ended, and it sleeps to wake no more?

OF ACTIVE RESIGNATION.

FEAR not the face of thy bemoanèd fate,
  Declare, " Thus art thou ; I accept thee now,"
  And then, no peevish fretfulness allow,
O'er many sorrows cease to meditate,
And do thy best to bear what thou didst hate.
  Behold ! the wrinkles on thy careworn brow
  Depart, serenity surrounds the vow,
And calm descends upon the long debate.

Thy nature to thy circumstance unfit
  Hath sorely frayed thy flesh ; resistance flings
  Corroding fetters o'er thy feeble wings.
But ah, the fire of fervent patience lit
  May fuse encircling or opposing things,
  And shape them to the mould the spirit brings.

UNCONSCIOUS INFLUENCE.

THE ripples come across the bay, and break
    In quick succession on the pebbly shore;
How faint th' impression each swift wave doth make
    Before it falls into the flood once more.
It leaves perchance, a shell or stone more worn,
    More polished or thrown forward into sight,
'Tis pleasant to the eye, but scarcely born
    Ere it retreats, as flies a flash of light.
Wave follows wave, as fresh thought follows thought,
    As life comes speeding after fading life;
How strange that each is with a purpose fraught,
    Though quite unconsciously it aids the strife
Of that great power which grinds rough places smooth,
Evolves from passion, love, so strong to soothe.

THE CELIBATE.

FROM childhood set apart, he has essayed
  With downcast eyes to avoid forbidden fruit;
  Yet gazing steadily at chiselled flute
Of massive pillar, a familiar shade
The presence of th' avoided one betrayed.
  His quivering eyelids, though his lips are mute,
  Bid him beware; for through the pulses shoot
Of tonsured priest, the love of man for maid!

Full many are there who have loved in vain,
  And for love's sake have lived their lives alone;
  But he,—and at the thought his heart will groan,—
Has been devoted to this scourging pain.
Enforced obedience finds it hard to gain
  The calmness of a choice which is its own.

OF MATURITY AND GROWTH.

The trees have clothed themselves most sumptuously
   In garments green of every varying shade;
   The blossoms have adorned the wooded glade,
The forming cones upon the boughs we see;
And now at this late hour, how fair to me
    Are those fresh shoots upon each tip displayed,
    Against the summer's dark'ning foliage laid,
Like fingers pointing to futurity.

Their growth gives promise for the coming spring
   Of ampler breadths of shade and wider bowers;
And from maturèd lips fresh thoughts should ring
   The advent of enlarged and freer powers;
For though the roots to earth must ever cling,
   The growing point into the ether towers.

THE SPECTRE OF WANT.

A DREADFUL shape is that of pallid Want!
It paralyses every noblest hope,
And narrows to the narrowest this life's scope;
Its famine-stricken limbs it seems to flaunt
Before the eyes of plenty; no fears daunt
　Its clutching fingers; quickly down the slope
　Of beggary to vice, e'en to the rope
It strides, and grows each day more wild and gaunt.
This haggard spectre knocking at the door
　Brings in its train the loss of home and friends,
　The death of effort, beauty forced to flee,
Fair honour dulled; for squalor evermore
　Means loss of shame; its scanty rags it rends,
　And sinks at worst beneath humanity.

NATURE.

Fair Nature smiles for happy youth, and scolds
   The fretful, frowning at them through their tears;
   To timid souls most heartless she appears,
Though braver children in her arms she folds,
And makes them happy on the breezy wolds,
   In sheltered gardens, where the good ship steers
   Its path across the sea. Pure minds she cheers,
And shapeless thoughts to lovely patterns moulds.

A goddess she, who plays her strenuous part
Without reluctance on the human heart;
To each law-breaker gives she that is his,
And takes no heed of idle sophistries;
She will not pause for end of long debates,
But heals her lovers, while her foes she hates!

JOHN HANCOCK.

(Naturalist. Died 11th October, 1890.)

O NATURE, he is dead who loved thee well,
    He leaves thy haunts, to lie upon thy breast,
    Thy swift-winged children guard his well-earned rest,
And chant Spring's birth songs and dark Winter's knell,
Unheeded by the ears which once could tell
    This note from that, and what the songster's quest,
    His plumage and his habits, where his nest,
On heathy hill-side or in wooded dell.

A man designed by Nature for herself,
With earnest purpose and contempt for pelf;
With patient brain to search her ways abstruse,
And clever hands grown skilful by long use;
Who heeded not the years already flown
Devoted to her cause, and hers alone!

SONNETS OF THE CITY.

I.

THE OLD CASTLE.

Thou dark and rugged relic of fierce days,
   If it be true that every surging sound
   Doth leave its trace, in striking and rebound,
How strangely pictured to a piercing gaze
Were thy grim masonry: what stirring lays
   Of border strife, of town-bred tumult found
   Upon thy walls would on the heart resound,
All mingled with the tones of prayer and praise;
For Sabbath bells and holy anthems ring
   Around thy battlements in war or peace;
Defacing stains of toil upon thee cling,
   And at thy feet the waves of life increase,
As one by one the generations sing
   Their songs of love and hate, which never cease!

II.

THE CATHEDRAL.

A LANDMARK thou; thy lantern sings above
   The crowded thoroughfares that hem thee in,
   A song of steadfast peace all men may win
By consecrating earthly life and love
To that great Power in which men live and move,
   Resistless in its hatred of all sin,
   And merciful to those who truly win
Their freedom from a narrow, selfish groove.
Thy shadow falls upon the busy mart,
   Reminding men of life's true aim and cause;
Thy stones are annals of the Northern heart,
   Its history is gathered round thy doors;
And thou a sacred sanction canst impart
   To joy or sorrow, when the heart adores.

III.

THE CENTRAL STATION.

THE pulsing life blood of the City pours
   Through thee its throbbing heart, unceasingly ;
Along thy gleaming ways the current roars
   In mingled tragedy and comedy.
Strange scenes from stranger lives, upon thy floors
   Without rehearsal acted, thou dost see;
And sad farewells of those who leave our shores,
   Bright marriage joy, and death's dark pageantry.

A link thou seemest in the lengthening chain
   Which binds this land to that, and man to man,
Until on one great Brotherhood no stain
   Of war remains, where once it wildly ran
A sleuth-hound, bringing ravage in its train.
   Free intercourse like thine is hatred's ban !

THE CHURCH OF THE DIVINE UNITY.

IV.

A MONUMENT art thou, of that long roll
  Of earnest men who fought on freedom's side :
Who strove to save th' aspiring, yearning soul
  From prisons of the past, and open wide
The Infinite ; that to its long-closed goal—
  The bosom of the Father—o'er the tide
Of raging billows which around it roll,
  The burthened heart may fly, and there abide !

A protest in the past ; for Faith to-day
  Thou standest firmly, full of fresh fire caught
From ever-growing, ever-widening thought,
Which onward, upward, cleaves its glorious way,
And will not, dare not, in the partial stay,
  Constrained to find the ONE each soul hath sought.

V.

THE PUBLIC LIBRARY.

THOU latest fledgling of fair Learning's brood,
  Thy ample chambers echo 'neath the tread
  Of those who had, in olden time been led
Into the ghastly field of war, where stood
The jealous barons, careless that the food
  Of wailing women, and weak children's bread,
  Depended on the men whom they have said
Shall fight unto the death! Not thine this mood;
Thou callest men to learn the arts of peace,
  Hast gathered on thy shelves a mighty store
  Of living words, which fell from men of yore,
The seed corn of a harvest, to increase
Through coming years, a thousand-fold and more,
  Until all bloodshed and fierce strife shall cease!

VI.

THE CEMETERY.

WITHIN thy grassy spaces, lowly laid
  Our loved ones lie; each grave's pathetic face
  Sun-kissed, acquires a silent, sadd'ning grace
With velvet moss or gorgeous blooms arrayed.
The signs of wealth or poverty displayed
  Are naught to those who wing through realms of space,
  And know no rest save in the close embrace
Of Him to whom aspiring spirits prayed.

E'en here alas, man's narrow love is found;
  But list, God laughs, His forces all deride
  These false divisions of mere place and pride.
In hallowed or unconsecrated mound
The useless body lies beneath the ground;
  No pall or pomp, th' immortal soul can hide.

VII.

THE REV. FRANK WALTERS.

O MAN of God! armed with a tongue of flame,
   To kindle in the soul a holy fire
   Of hopeful courage, and of pure desire
To do the work of Him from whom it came:
Thou bidst men cease from deeds and thoughts of shame,
   And shake from off their feet earth's clinging mire,
   Unto a nobler, better life aspire,
The life of selfless love and stainless fame.

The Universe the home of the Most High,
   The earth a temple when the heart is pure,
   Eternal life a promise, strong and sure,
And God, a Father to His children nigh,
Who hears the wand'rer's first repentant cry;
   These are thy message,—men's sick souls to cure.

NATURAL AND SUPERNATURAL.

FAMILIAR scenes and faces rouse no fear,
   And that which all men say gives no distress,
   The well-worn garments lose uneasiness,
And daily rounds quite natural appear.
Within a silenced room incline your ear
   To voices from afar; then pause to guess
   The horror which had fallen for far less
On those who knew not whence came sounds so clear.
The unfamiliar supernatural seems,
   Strange, weird, and painful to the shrinking sight,
   It haunts the darkness of the gaping night
With vague, ungrasped, and unaccustomed dreams.
But on the shudd'ring world a new sun beams,
   For Law and Love, on every place pour light!

OF TWILIGHT AND MELANCHOLY.

An hour there is between the day and dark,
   When summer foliage and the fairest flowers
   Look grey and sombre as the evening lowers,
Until a scintillating, quiv'ring spark
Shines out o'er undulating hills, to mark
   The passing of the gloaming into night.
   A peaceful time it seems, though never bright,
The plaintive nightingale supplants the lark;
And moments come to every heart when joy
   Gives place to melancholy's quiet thought,
   When past and present to one hue are brought,
And jokes or merry quips are apt to cloy,
For in life's shadows memory finds employ,
   While with deep meaning spoken words are fraught.

IS LOVE ETERNAL?

DOTH aught last through the long eternity
 Of progress which awaits a conscious soul?
 Or as it nears its final, long-sought goal
Do lesser hopes entirely cease to be?
Doth Love remain when all else fades away,
 Inextricably woven into life,
 Steadfast and strong when death and change are rife,
The joy of future as of present day?

Why ask such questions, O thou restless heart,
 Is Love of clay to perish on the earth?
  The passions of the flesh must all expire
  When dust returns unto its native mire;
 But selfless Love may dare the dangerous birth,—
Called death;— for Love is man's most God-like part.

IN CLOUDLAND.

Across the pearly arch of eve outspread
   A pair of Seraph wings were lifted high,
   No form between them could my eyes descry,
No face with friendly glance; and soon the red
Of sunset caught the snowy plumes, and shed
   From tip to tip a rosy hue, to die
   In burning blushes o'er the western sky.
"A Seraph seeks the earth to-night," I said,
" Who shall be counted fit his face to see,
   Or feel his hand withdraw from wrath and wrong ? "
They laughed,—the others,—gaily mocking me,
   But trees took up a soft, angelic song,
   And bending, rustling, murmured it along
The gleaming river, gliding to the sea.

A DAWNING FAITH.

THE ancient faiths are crumbling to decay,
   Each saint is tott'ring in his time-worn niche;
   The seer, no longer branded as a witch,
Proclaims her oracles by light of day;
And rash, irrev'rent children rudely play
   With ball, and cross, and crescent; all of which
   Are sacred symbols given to enrich
The inner life, to teach men how to pray.
The outward forms are dying; but incline
   Your ear unto the living, throbbing hearts
   Of toiling men in crowded, busy marts.
You gaze astonished, for they answer thine!
What is that pulse, so human, yet divine?
   The sense that ALL men of ONE LIFE are parts.

PRAISE IS BLAME!

THE dewdrop forms its perfect glitt'ring sphere,
   And nestles in the hollow of a flower,
   Content to lie there hidden the brief hour
Of its short life; nor does it e'er appear
To seek applause of fellow dewdrops near,
   For each fair orb is gifted with full power
   To form itself, and none need darkly glower
To see the others pure and round and clear.
And man is only praised because the lame,
   The deaf, the dull, the coarse are of his kind,
   Because endued with thinking, choosing mind,
A few shine out against the many's shame.
So sunny praise involves its shadow, blame;
   For why laud sight, if never man were blind?

THE TRANSFORMATION OF PAIN.

GAUNT Pain, with sunken cheeks and closèd lips,
　Stands weeping, groaning, rending her scant locks :
　A writhing world with her wild eyes she mocks,
Exuberance of thoughtless youth she nips,
And flaws the cup the holy martyr sips.
　The feeble body quails beneath her shocks,
　And backward, forward, seeking ease it rocks,
In vain attempt to avoid her scourging whips.

But see, a miracle! Her lips long sealed
　At last are opening into tender speech ;
　Her tears of sympathy begin to teach
A sense of human oneness, which hath healed
Full many a scar beneath its shelt'ring shield ;
　And Pain, transformed to Pity, smiles for each.

AUTUMN.

The Autumn leaves are falling, falling fast,
   And gusty winds are driving them away
   In stormy earnest, or in sportive play,
Until they find a sheltered nook at last
Where round the mould'ring heaps decay may cast
   Her blighting arms, to press them day by day
   More closely to her breast, and whisp'ring say,
"All dead! their fleeting hours of life are past."

But are they dead? Their loveliness 'tis true,
   Their shapes and hues are gone for aye; but look
How Mother Earth absorbs them to renew
Her energies, from which their life they drew.
   Why call it Death to fall back whence they took
   Their being? "Changed, not dead," says Nature's
      book.

OF CHILDREN.

INTO a solemn household came a child,
And all was changed by his soft, chubby hand,
Which ruled with rod of iron; his demand
For love and care, for merry play, beguiled
The stately mother till she gaily smiled.
    The nursery floor became a magic land,
    Where a promiscuous, ever-changing band
Of angels, beasts, and fairies wandered wild.

Behind that sunshine a dark shadow lurks,
    For there are little ones whose unshod feet
    Know nothing softer than the stony street.
The pen to picture their condition shirks!
    What can be done, O Mothers, to make sweet
    The lives of children whom men's curses greet?

OF FAILURE AND PROGRESS.

I CHOSE the rose, and laid it on my breast;
   Its beauty filled my senses with delight,
   But e'en before the advent of the night
Its withered petals, no more gaily dressed
Fell one by one; nor dared I lift them, lest
     The others followed. Did I choose aright
     To take that scented blossom frail and bright?
Was that the noblest choice, the purest, best?

Beside the flower of passion, sweet and gay,
   The scentless everlasting raised its head:
But I, a mortal, chose the passing day,
   Nor looked beyond the portal of the dead.
Shall I for ever choose the lower way,
   Or taught by failure, climb where it hath led?

LOVING AND BELOVED.

To love is hard, when love is unreturned.
But being loved is far, far harder yet,
Therein lies weariness and vain regret
For all that might have been, had true love burned
With equal flame in either heart, and earned
   The double power of those twin currents set
   In one broad channel. Now the stones scarce wet,
The stream is by the least obstruction turned.

O God! how shall both hearts be satisfied
   In time to come, if this can only know
   A bliss which from that other heart shall flow?
Yet in that heart no bond is ratified,
   Nor doth it long for love, more than the snow
   Doth long for sunshine which shall make it flow!

THE EARTH.

Consider well the earth, its light and shade,
The varied beauties everywhere displayed;
   The wild luxuriance of its tropic clime,
   With wealth of blossoms and deep beds of slime;
The temperate zone, in verdant green arrayed,
With starry hosts upon its meadows laid;
   The rugged mountains, lifting crowns sublime
   Of hoary locks which know no summer time;
The frozen circle, where the ground dismayed
Forgets to bloom, so keen is winter's raid;
   The mystic ocean, whose deep currents chime
   Against great hills no foot of man may climb.
Shall God disdain the glories He hath made,
Who every atom in His balance weighed?

SHAKESPEARE.

IMPARTIAL art thou, as the teeming earth,
  On which swarm creatures vile and gay and good;
With sympathy o'erflowing, scorn, or mirth
  Men's heart's stripped bare before thy glances stood.
The cup of life with bold hand thou dost fill,
  Nor dost withhold the fatal poisoned drop
Which poured therein, all love and peace must kill,
  And yet far short of license dost thou stop:
For on himself the murderer's cruel knife
  Relentlessly returns to rend his flesh,
And where vile lust and treachery are rife,
  The traitors fall at last in their own mesh.
Robustest son of a most glorious age,
No feeble palliations stain thy page.

JOHN MILTON.

Set high above the misty realms of sight,
　Thou hast created a Titanic sphere;
Hast darkened the dark shadows of the night,
　And deepened the deep hells of abject fear;
And yet 'tis strange, thy Satan, this world's blight,
　Is grandly human too when he comes near;
He will not bow before a tyrant's might,
　And reigns in Hell to keep his conscience clear!

O Poet, by thy blindness set apart
　To things impalpable thou drawest nigh;
Such fame as thine no mere success can buy,
It is the load-star of the struggling heart
　That longs above all petty strife to fly,
　And must its work accomplish ere it die.

ROBERT BROWNING.

UNMUSICAL, grotesque sometimes thy lays,
  And yet how deeply dost thou probe the heart!
  Thou lay'st thy finger on its inmost smart
With healing magic; and the soul arrays
Reformèd forces in more subtile ways,
  Upon more elemental, stronger lines;
  Deep down into life's less exhausted mines
Thou darest, winning ore for future days.

Thy thoughts now saturate the minds of those
  Who read them not: from thy deep well they drink,
  Although of thee they never pause to think,
Nay, deem themselves perchance, thy bitter foes!
Upon the past and future thy hands close,
  And *that* to *this* most firmly dost thou link.

THE RISING TIDE.

A SURGING sea there is within the breast,
　Which ebbs and flows, and breaks upon the shore
　Of silence.   Ah, the coming waves implore
To understand their meaning, and find rest.
The frothing foam upon th' uplifted crest
　Which hurries on to break with thundrous roar
　Upon the shining strand, and fall once more
Into the ocean, puts life to the test.

And if it gain one inch as yet unwon,
　Or learn one secret buried in the sand,
Its life-work it has nobly, truly done,
　And paved the way for the advancing band
Which shall accomplish that which it begun;
　Till one by one, life's secrets open stand.

A MAGNETIC PERSONALITY.

He enters; small frivolities decline,
  A healthy movement, as of mountain breeze,
  Arouses slumb'ring earnestness, and frees
The guarded tongue to utter thoughts divine.
His gestures grant unspoken prayers; like wine
  His flowing words give strength, and his decrees
  Are forming now the future that he sees;
Through clouds and darkness day begins to shine.
He laughs; despairing souls feel loads of woe
  Mysteriously removed; the atmosphere
Is cleansed of cobwebs, men aspire to go
  On herculean tasks forgetting fear,
  Contemptible excuses disappear,
For all desire the noblest things they know.

THE GIFT OF HOPE.

The orphaned maiden dreams that she shall wed,
   That solitude and sorrow both shall cease.
Th' unhappy wife is fain to lay her head
   Within the grave; beyond it she sees peace.
And weeping autumn, old and witherèd,
   Feels at her heart a promise of increase,
While shrouded winter stirs in her cold bed,
   And longs of life to try another lease.

The greatest gift that e'er to man was sent
   Is Hope! She looks beyond the present hour,
   Above the thorn gives promise of the flower.
She sees the raging storm-clouds' fury spent,
And whispers that these pressing woes are meant
   To prove the spirit, and evolve its power.

THE POINT OF VIEW.

SEEN from afar the Master's canvas shows
  A blurred and formless stretch of dun grey sky;
No message there from Nature for the woes
  Of sorrowing men, who pass it dully by.
But draw thou nearer; see where daylight grows;
  And nearer still, till here and there an eye
Peers from the flakelets forming into rows,
  With outspread pinions, lifted as to fly.
Then stand awhile with fixèd, steadfast gaze;
  Ah, now the clouds take shape, and cherub heads
With parted lips sweet hallelujahs raise.
Their lifted faces catch celestial rays
  Descending from above; the heavenly weds
The earthly, and transforms thy anxious days.

SUBTERRANEAN CURRENTS.

A MIGHTY river runs beneath the ground
    Unguessed, until in some abysmal deep
    It leaves its hidden bed perforce, to sweep
'Twixt horrent rocks, which echoing, resound
With fearful roar to every leap and bound.
    The faintest twilight falls upon its face,
    Where blindly rushing, raging with wild grace,
It plunges back to darkness most profound.

And are there none, of all our humankind,
    With subterranean currents running fast,
        Which flow with harmless swiftness till they reach
        The narrow cleft of unaccustomed speech?
    Into that seething channel forced at last,
The fierceness of the torrent who shall bind?

TO EACH, HIS OWN.

"Why must I stay upon the dreary ground
And suffer thus? 'Tis fairer up above,
In those clear spaces where no fogs are found,
And nearer to the sky light cloudlets rove;
Where gloomy shadows fall not, and around
The arch of blue an ample roof must prove;
Where steady lights in darkest night abound,
And life is purity and peace and love."

Thy beings law demands that thou shalt stay
Upon the earth while thou art still of clay;
Like gravitates to like, and thou mayst choose
The noblest or the worst of earth to lose;
And when thou'rt fit for fairer realms than this,
Translated shalt thou be to higher bliss.

IS THERE ANY END?

The tottering infant looks across the floor,
   His one desire to reach the arms he sees
Outstretched to welcome him : he fails once more,
   Yet nothing save to walk upright will please
Th' ambitious child. Within an open door
   There stands a youth, who envies every breeze
That flits at will to some far distant shore,
   And till he follow he can know no ease.
An aged man looks onward still, and longs
   For fresh experience in another sphere,
To cross the boundary, redress old wrongs
   In ampler life, undewed by sorrow's tear :
He strains to catch the echo of new songs,
   And bids the earth adieu without a fear.

"HE THAT LOVETH HIS LIFE SHALL LOSE IT."

Go, garner thou thy store in well-locked barns,
    And keep thy thoughts within thy silent lips;
    Venture not forth when frosty winter nips,
And hide thy gold in deep, dark mountain tarns.
Keep all thou canst, let no man share thy gains,
    Let no man know thou hast a beating heart;
    In all the work of life, take thou no part,
Dry no sad tears, alleviate no pains.
And then, what art thou? Living all alone,
And petrifying slowly into stone,
    No humanising accents from thee fall;
No fallow field beneath thy care grows green;
'Twere better that thy life had never been,
    For thou art NOTHING! Judgment worst of all!

OF EDUCATION BY CHOICE.

A CHOICE of youth may lead to long regret
  For false direction by its impulse given
  Unto the past, which then is rudely riven
From life's small whole, to leave it smaller yet,
With little time to learn or to forget.
  And yet, perchance the future had been lost
  Except for bitter sorrow failure cost,
Arousing hopes for ever higher set.

Some grossness of the nature made that choice
  Imperative, to cleanse away impurity
  Contracted by the soul, that its maturity
On loftier level, with more even poise
May stand and speak aloud with prophet voice;
  A squandered past, the staff of its security.

SUFFER, AND BE STRONG.

THE trees are pruned that they may bear much fruit,
And storm and cold make strong the northern heart:
Then rouse thee, suff'rer, bravely do thy part,
In life's tear-watered garden strike thy root.
See all the martyrs, mutilated, flayed,
Burnt at the stake; yet their faith never failed,
The tortured flesh it was, at most, which quailed,
And these are they who walk in white array'd.
The heroes of all ages, who endured
But would not stoop to say one word untrue,
From scattered graves speak yet, weak heart, to you
Of fruitful blessings their sad lives secured.
They smiled in persecution's fire for Right,
And died in arms against the tyrant Might.

OF PRESENTIMENTS.

THE air before a storm is dull and still,
   Yet restlessly the leaves sway to and fro
   Wavering from side to side. Some coming woe
I augur from the deadly, numbing chill
Of this sad heart, which once was wont at will
   With ease to rise o'er trials, such as go
   And come, from whence and whither none can know.
I turn from hope to fear, from good to ill,
For clouds brood heavily along the West,
   As lies my future cowering 'neath a fear,
     A shapeless doubt, and far extending dread.
The lightning flash shall be a welcome guest,
   To rend the growing gloom, and leave it clear,
     E'en though it strike my heart and leave it dead!

OF EXISTENCE AND LIFE.

Is toiling life so sad as some men think,
  So steeped in pain, so gloomy and distressed?
Believe me, no! Stand on a river's brink
  And watch the water gliding, then compressed.
Which grinds the corn? The sluggish, shallow stream,
  Loitering 'twixt lovely meads in verdure dressed,
Or yonder narrowed mill-race you see gleam,
  Resisting, tossing, rearing its white crest?

The fretted water, turned against its will
  By some disposing power that shapes its end,
    Through pressure rises to its work at length.
Shall man exist without th' exultant thrill
  That honest labour and great effort send
    Along each nerve, arousing latent strength.

IN OXFORD.

To stand within these ancient, echoing halls,
   And tread these foot-worn cloisters, cool and dark,
   Or meditate in high-walled gardens, mark
The hand of Time laid softly on the walls
Which sheltered generations; this appals
   The eager heart, and bids it use its spark
   Of life with honesty, to light the bark
That sails a moment, ere death's curtain falls.

Yes, man is small compared with all mankind,
   Not e'en so much as one hewn stone close set
   In these grey Colleges, and yet,—and yet,—
Each stone must keep its place, that it may bind
The whole to its perfection: so I find
   Each life is needed, and my eyes are wet.

DISUSE AND DECAY.

THE unused limb must shrivel and decay,
   And a neglected soul as surely pines,
   Contracts, grows dim, no longer clearly shines,
Then flickers, and fades out. The god-like ray
Of spirit vision vanishes away,
   And though the lamp remain, the light is lost,
   Contentment gained at th' overwhelming cost
Of that divine unrest which once held sway.

The passing soul, departing, gives no groan,
   Its agonies grow feebler as it faints,
     And darkness settles down where light once reigned.
The furrows fallow lie, with grain unsown,
   While foul malaria the still air taints;
     A slothful heaven of selfish peace is gained!

LIMITED AND LIMITLESS.

WITHIN the narrow compass of the real,
   As in a splendid palace, mankind dwells,
   With space to live and breathe, and many wells
From which to drink; but needful for his weal
Are boundless heights and depths of the ideal,
   Exhaustless as the ether which outswells
   Into a seeming arch, whose vastness quells
All limitations to the truth unleal.

The future, looming large and unconfined,
   And free from trammels of a fixèd past,
     Gives ample breathing room for boundless hope,
     Elastic, radiant, far beyond the scope
   Of one short life to grasp, or to hold fast;
Illimitable as Eternal mind!

OF PASSION.

Fierce Passion, like the heat of tropic clime,
  Awakes the latent powers within the heart
  To sudden growth ; from hidden deeps upstart
The poisonous weed, or gorgeous crown sublime
Of fragrant flowers ; the soft, melodious chime
  Of whirring insect life its drowsy part
  Takes up harmoniously ; or lightning's dart
To devastate the toil of previous time.
In that upheaval each soul brings to birth,
  According to its nature, good or ill
  In wild profusion, nor is sated till
For weal or woe, its torrent to the earth
Is poured resistlessly in deeds of worth,
  Or hideous crimes with horror hearts to fill.

THE NINETEENTH CENTURY.

This is the time for living souls to live,
   For generous hearts their wealth of love to pour
   Into an ocean widening evermore
To hold the utmost measure man can give.
And this the age for earnest minds to seek
   Secure foundations for fast-growing thought;
   To ask, and ask again, is strongly taught,
And what each finds, with courage must he speak.
Of freedom, glorious glimpses gleam and glance
   Across the eager eyes oped wide to see
   The promise of a grander century
When all shall march where now a few advance.
Although we see it not, our lives to-day
Are paving, ill or well, the widening way.

AFTER RAIN.

AFTER RAIN.

How pure the air when ceases summer rain,
  And day's bright atmosphere is crystal clear;
The birds in ecstasy arise again
  On quiv'ring wings, that almost still appear.
Each living thing lifts up its head anew,
  The sun shines out, and clouds pass quickly by;
Our tears are shed, and hope springs up to sue
  For life and love, where sorrow longed to die.

Thank God for tears! It is the silent grief
  That eats like rust into a sullen soul,
    Or flashes swift, dry fire, to devastate
    With dangerous lightning of despair and hate.
  When torrents fall, away the storm-clouds roll
And sunshine gilds each shining, rain-washed leaf.

A SELFISH PARADISE.

They live within an Eden full of joy,
  By day they wander in its leafy glades,
  At night lie down to sleep in grateful shades,
Their youthful hearts are full of glad employ,
The cares of life pass by without annoy.
  She envies not the dancing, singing maids,
  And he breast-high in rapture's river wades,
No serpent glides,—it seems,—peace to destroy.

They fare not forth beyond the shining gate,
  And take no heed of distant, wailing cries.
  She cares not that the orphaned maiden dies
Untended, that wild hearts and hungry wait
Outside, for falling crumbs of her glad state.
  But ah! the longest summer quickly flies.

DRIVEN OUT!

FATE lingers ere she strikes the final blow;
And when the boisterous breath of winter falls,
Its biting edge their tender flesh appals;
For hardship unprepared, yet must they go
To meet the penetrating, drifting snow.
　For warmth and shelter each dismayed heart calls,
　But closed is Paradise, and round its walls
A swollen torrent swirls with gath'ring flow.

Shall they succumb to this severer clime,
　Or braced to nobler effort by the blast,
　Their selfishness for ever from them cast,
And rise to truer life, and more sublime,
Leave Eden-gate, and bravely thither climb
　Where love attains true blessedness at last?

OF GENIUS AND HUMILITY.

How shall a gifted man be arrogant?
   As well the lighthouse of its place be proud,
   And scorn the rushing and excited crowd
Of waves, which roaring round it, seethe and pant.
His lamp is lighted; and 'tis his to lift
   A steady front, to cast his beams afar,
   That mariners in danger on the bar
No longer on unwarnèd rocks may drift.

Capacity is God's one measure used
   To test the life-work of the small or great;
   For what man *can*, he *must* do soon or late;
And he who boasts his power has most abused
His gifts. Shall widest ocean be elate
   That it is deep; a boon to rills refused?

THE TELEGRAPH WIRES.

ACROSS a grey and heavy Autumn sky
    A fleeting glimpse is caught of phantom wires,
Enveloped in a mass of clouds they lie
    And scarcely clearer than half-formed desires.
I stay to listen with abated breath
    As breezes through those far threads faintly sigh :
What words of hope or dread, of life or death,
    O'erhead from heart to heart unnoticed fly?
So slight and subtle e'en material things
    Need be to annihilate dividing space!
Why need we wonder then that mind has wings
    Which flash with lightning speed from place to place,
That soul its fibres o'er the dark gulf flings
    To hold a loved one in a fond embrace.

THE SPRING-TIME OF LOVE.

As each returning Spring awakes the flowers
   And whispers with its sweet, reviving breath,
   "Arouse, and bloom again, it was not death
But sleep which held thee," and her gentle showers
Transform gaunt woods to happy lovers' bowers,
   Which echo back the sacred, solemn vows
   Oft spoken 'neath the interlacing boughs
By youth and maid, in life's divinest hours;
So on the wintry heart Love breathes awhile,
   And stirs it to its innermost recess,
   Awaking strange and yearning restlessness
To reach the soft, warm air. Love can beguile
The dead to life; his eyes and tender smile
   Work miracles of new-born happiness.

NEW YEAR'S EVE.

THE sacred past, the unknown future, link
  Together on the eve of New Year's Day:
Last year, the year to come,—we pause, and think
  What that has been, what this shall have to say;
  And while the eyes and lips are sparkling, gay,
The heart stands trembling on the very brink
  Of tears, to know how many are away.
A silent health to absent friends we drink.

A darkness lies around the future's flight,
  And hides her pathway from our eager eyes;
One step before her flashes a faint light,
  One thread across her busy finger lies.
No man may know if she be dark or bright,
  Upon her lips unbroken silence lies.

A TRAGEDY.

An honoured man, and splendidly arrayed,
   The envy of a thousand lesser lights,
   But ah! look in where now his conscience bites
And bids him lay aside this false parade.
Devotion to his office has decayed
   Through changing thought; within himself he fights
   To keep, if possible, the dear delights
Of pomp and place. Decision is delayed.
Successful, yet how often hath he pressed
   A hand upon his heart the pulse to still
   That throbs so painfully against his will.
A prisoner at the bar knows more of rest
Than this great cleric, flattered and carressed,
   Who starves his soul, and reads, "Thou shalt not
     kill."

OF SEEMING WASTE.

THE forest flower, the heather on the hill,
　The teeming insect life that swarms the air,
What purpose do these serve? Their beauty rare
Seems wasted, for blooms die ungathered still;
No hand hath plucked them perfume to distil,
　No voice is heard to say the flies are fair,
　Nor each for other do they seem to care,
But come and go, and meet and part, at will.
This wild profusion seems sometimes but waste;
　And yet, it may be, we are far too dull
　　To see their subtle influences start.
Th' Omniscient has no need for any haste,
　Nor doth he wish that MAN should all things cull!
　　God sees the whole, where mortals see a part.

THE INDESTRUCTIBILITY OF HOPE.

The nesting birds in Spring sing merrily,
    And mate with busy note calls to his mate,
"These hours are sweet, but summer soon shall be,
    For that more glorious time 'tis hard to wait."
Wild Autumn hurries on to strip the tree,
    And with her rough wet hand to desecrate
The home; all unfulfilled the prophecy
    Of perfect pleasure, though the year grows late.

Yet hope survives! In this life man may fail,
    His cherished plans be trodden in the dust,
His young ideals wither and grow pale,
    And still assurèdly he puts his trust
    In joy to come: he feels the future must
Ope wide the gate, his spirit longs to assail!

MATTER AND SPIRIT.

DULL matter lies content in its fixed place,
　　No thrilling current through its essence runs;
Not yet the subtle and refining grace
　　Of rousing, restless soul, its visage suns.
But breathe the Breath of Life into the clod,
　　And spirit stirring, strains with opened eyes
To pierce the trammels of its narrow sod,
　　And flutter nearer to the azure skies.
To work will it desire, to teach, be taught,
　　But ne'er to live as though it were not come
From warmer climes; ah, thence it surely brought
　　Its snatches of sweet song. Soul is not dumb,
For rising feebly on its half-grown wings,
An exile's home-sick melodies it sings.

OF HEROISM.

GREAT heroes have been praised for warlike deeds,
    Philanthropists for courage to be just,
    The white-robed priest because he puts his trust
In God the Father, who e'en ravens feeds.
In every country, and of all the creeds,
    Prophets and martyrs waging war 'gainst lust
    Have been revered; by later ages thrust
Into the niches superstition breeds.
But he who lives a stunted, quiet life,
    Heroic in self-sacrifice, too great
      For his dull prison house, how deep and dire
The suff'ring he has borne ere eager strife
    Could end in noble patience, strong to wait.
      Who sings his steadfast courage in that fire?

HIDDEN.

Throw open, silent soul, the pearly gate
Of thy dark mind, and let the moving air,
The vivifying sun, play freely there,
For unexplorèd wonders hidden wait
A friendly hand the gloom to dissipate,
   And bring to light its secrets strange and rare,
   Which now dense drapery of dust must wear;
The mourning garment of the desolate.

Thou heedest not; ah, thou art silent still!
   No words hast thou to turn the rusty key
     Of that dark fortress where no footstep falls
     With answering echo on the massy walls.
   Mute lips impassable, imprison thee
Alone, in dungeons dreary, dark, and chill.

THE WAGES OF SIN.

I.

Twice o'er Sin pays thee, if thou kiss her hand;
   She gives thee life, where haunting spectres race
To lay their soiling fingers on the brand
   Thy lips have taken from that dread embrace.
Remorse, then fear, dark secrecy demand,
   And scorpion whips surround thee, for disgrace
With mocking smile and scornful eye doth stand
   To tear thee at a word from thy loved place.

With one hand Sin gives life unknown before;
   And with the other death! She takes from thee
Fair innocence that probes thought to the core,
   Majestic in its fearlessness, and free.
And thou art ferried to another shore,
   Where many phantoms menace threateningly.

THE WAGES OF SIN.

II.

Upon the brink thou standest long to mourn
  The smiling landscape, once thy fair estate,
By swiftly running river from thee torn.
  No boatman backward plies; why dost thou wait
With fruitless tears and aspect so forlorn
  Upon the abhorrèd deed to meditate,
And curse the bitter day, the cheerless dawn,
  For which unwillingly thy heart doth wait?

March on, O man, in sober, chastened guise,
Well armed by this first fall against surprise;
  So through disaster wisdom shall gain strength,
Some safeguard for the future to devise,
  And bring thee to a citadel at length
Where stalwart purity all ill defies.

SUSPENSE.

The sword is dangling from a lofty roof,
    Suspended by a frail, elastic thread;
And he who sits beneath looks not aloof,
    Although intensely conscious, sick with dread.
Against such agony no gold is proof,
    And fate disdains to spare the crownèd head,
In weaving her mysterious warp and woof,
    Fair purple raiment rends she to a shred.

The shudd'ring flesh endures the coming wound
    A hundredfold; and that dark, threatened woe,
Through every nerve to torture pitch attuned,
    Upon a rising scale strikes blow on blow.
But see! the sword has fallen; he has swooned,
    Suspense is o'er, and healing forces flow!

AMONG THE HILLS.

I WAKE, and lo! the sparkling air seems dumb,
  So deep the peace that broods upon the hills;
  But casements opened wide let in fresh rills
Of blissful sound. From noisy city come,
In place of industry's gigantic hum,
  A murmur of the bees the garden fills,
  And mountain calm upon the heart distils
In soothing dews, till carking care grows numb.

'Tis life's elixir to leave towns behind
  And revel in a place of crowded peaks;
Each well-known outline eagerly to find,
  And press the lips to Summer's blushing cheeks.
Up, up, past beds of bracken, where the wind
  Across the bursting heather softly speaks.

VICARIOUS SUFFERING.

THOUGH every man his meed of pain endures,
  Not all have felt the joy beneath the grief,
  For which the longest agony seems brief,
So true the satisfaction it assures.
A power there is in suff'ring that allures
  The sternest and the hardest to its side;
  A dying word suffices to ope wide
The long-locked soul, and pour in oil that cures.

Then die is faith. Nay, harder, choose to live!
  Thy pain upon the altar bravely lay;
  Unselfish joy is thine, if thou canst say
" My pangs for him, or her, I freely give."
  Long tongues of light shoot from celestial day
  Their roseate hues to cast upon thy way.

THE DISCOVERER.

HE stands with lifted taper in the midst
Of dark mysterious worlds, and strains to see
   Beyond the circlet's haloed radiancy.
Titanic facts he holds with iron wrist,
Until their lifeless lips to life are kissed,
   Their features limned for all futurity.
   Content he is to live most sparingly
If but one link the less of truth be missed!

One atom understood, one inch annexed,
   One higher harmony, a lifetime sought,
   Hath he by patient toil with ardour bought;
One secret opened, one thought less perplexed,
One step prepared for him who cometh next.
   He sleeps in peace; his life was not for naught.

CARNIVAL.

In holiday attire, with sparkling eyes
   The young fare forth a Carnival to enjoy;
   In glitt'ring shows the senses find employ,
O'er seething multitudes day swiftly flies ;
Exhilaration wave on wave doth rise,
   Till fast and furious grows the fun, and masks
   Are donned to cover o'er mysterious tasks,
And merriment in boisterous laughter dies.
Processions pass, fair flowers are wildly thrown,
   Unearthly forms glide stealthily, disguised,
   The sober citizen is soon despised,
And Order yields to wild Misrule her throne.
The dancing masquers every care disown,
   And hour by hour are gayer games devised.

LENT.

But list! The Minster chimes ring midnight. Lent
   Begins, with days of penitence enforced,
   The heated brain, where pleasure swiftly coursed,
Is aching on a pillow, or down bent
Beneath a lofty dome. The air is rent
   No more with madd'ning ecstasy or song,
   Dark words, instead, of agony and wrong
With piteous prayers and dull regrets are blent.
For this year,—or this life,—the masquerade
   Is over; treading softly, strive thou well,
   That on thy heart the coming advent-bell
May echo gladly. O prepare to wade
The stream 'twixt years,—or lives,—all undismayed,
   Full glad that Lenten penance on thee fell.

CONVERSION.

We walk perforce upon an upward track,
   Our faces backward turned to glance below;
   With stumbling and unseeing steps we go,
As to the sharp embrace of torture's rack.
To this side, then to that, we vainly tack,
   And progress is uncertain, painful, slow,
   For duty knows not ardour's cheerful glow,
And from the valley voices call us back.

But hark! at noon a clear, resounding note
   Far, far above, falls through the stilly air;
   And eager eyes are turned to scan with care
The rocky incline, whence the accents float.
   Th' abyss forgotten, dangerous steps we dare;
   To willing feet the steep ascent grows fair.

A REVERIE.

She sat beneath the hawthorn's scented shade,
Her golden head against its rugged trunk,
In day-dreams of the future deeply sunk,
With spotless robes of innocence arrayed.
The summer breezes, softly passing, swayed
    The blossom-laden branches; white showers fell
    Upon the upturned face, and broke the spell,
Recalling wand'ring fancies whence they strayed.

What were the thoughts behind that dream-rapt face,
    What hopes, what visions crowded on her sight?
Saw she a silver thread, by which to trace
    Her way through cloudy day and moonless night,
Or have her wishes cankered roots, to blight
    Her beauty, and destroy her guileless grace?

OF BLINDNESS.

WITHIN the arching hollow of the dark,
   Resounding on the sight-stripped, quickened ear,
   Fall many steps and voices. Ah, how drear
To list the rising of the happy lark,
To feel the warmth of summer sun, and mark
   The fall of ripples on the strand, and hear
   The rustle of the giant limes quite near,
Yet never see of beauty, e'en one spark !

Ah yes, 'tis sad to live with closèd eyes,
   But sadder far, that blindness of the soul
   Which hears the tide of life for ever roll,
And feels the heat that glowing hope applies
To rouse a frost-bound world, yet helpless lies,
   Awaiting guidance to its unseen goal.

THE EVOLUTION OF WOMANHOOD.

I.

WOMAN a living soul! The savage laughs,
    So wild the thought. What, she, the slavish squaw,
    Who humbly stands within the wigwam door
And bending, hands her lord the cup he quaffs.
The woman has no soul; no epitaphs,
    No tales, no songs of all his great tribe's store
    Are said, or sung, for her who lives no more,
And then again in utter scorn he laughs!

But she who hears the words, knows what is said,
    And in her heart a Something strangely stirs
    As softly as a zephyr o'er the furze.
It whispers, "Thou, and he whom thou hast wed,
Shall never die." The stern chief turns his head,
    Gazes on her brightened face, and wonders!

THE EVOLUTION OF WOMANHOOD.

II.

Woman a living soul! The brave knight yields
  The point: benignly grants that greatest gift
  Of immortality, and deigns to lift
The woman from the earth. Yet still he wields
A mighty power. "'Tis man," he says, "who shields
  The weakling from the dangers of the way,
  From all the heat and burthen of the day,
That she may shelter in his shady fields."

But she, who sees fair strangers come, and go,
  From distant lands, or to some warmer clime,
  Who hears of oceans vast, of hills sublime,
With summits clad in pure, eternal snow,
  Grows weary of those groves and longs to climb
To heights where fresher breezes freely blow.

THE EVOLUTION OF WOMANHOOD.

III.

WOMAN a living soul! Thank God, we say,
 No woman now need ask that boon to share ;
 She claims her right that crown of thorns to wear,
To lift the cross, to tread the rugged way
Which leads from earth, to pure, eternal day;
 In truth's great quest her earnest part to bear,
 From falsehood its beguiling mask to tear,
Her part right well upon this plane to play.

Unsullied womanhood, with lifted eyes,
Stands gazing steadily on opening skies ;
 Before that purity the proudest bow.
No scornful lip her worshippers defies,
She listens calmly to their clam'rous cries,
 And bids them live as those bound by a vow.

A SUNBEAM.

As when a sunbeam lights a gloomy vale,
   And gilds the common haunts of every day;
Or pierces through the wierd and weary wail
   Of sighing wind, with bright and cheery ray;
Or penetrates a dark tarn's misty veil
   Forcing a smile upon its face to play;
Or follows on the storm-cloud's inky trail,
   To chase its sullen sadness quite away;
So on my heart a gleam of purest joy
   Breaks through the atmosphere of doubt and dread,
   And flickers round my bowed and aching head.
It whispers in my ear, "Rise now, employ
   Thy God-given powers; thy dark way boldly tread."
   I rise, and lo! the stormy clouds have fled!

THEN AND NOW.

IN bygone days I carolled like a bird,
    And thought to penetrate life's secret core;
    Deep draughts I drank of sweet delight, and saw
Prismatic hues around; light fancies whirred
In sunny places, nor was I deterred
    From explorations on the slippery shore
    Of unrestrained imagination's lore,
For fear remained a pulseless, lifeless word.
But now, my hand goes out into a realm
    So vast, I feel no thrill of air returned
    From any boundary, and I have learned
To fear the infinite, lest it o'erwhelm
    The individuality that burned
A beacon for the pilot at the helm.

OF IMMORTALITY.

Why wait for an immortal life, till Death
   Has laid his hand upon a life like this?
   The future will not bring *created* bliss
Or new desires, through failure of the breath.
The child exists before he breathes the air;
   Could he inspire at all, save that he lives?
   And only in the measure this day gives
'Tis possible to-morrow's life to share.
Bestir thyself; draw in deep draughts of thought,
   Of love, and sympathy; awake, and know
   That here, and now, the heavenly waters flow
From founts perennial, waiting to be sought.
Immortal life is not mere length of days,
But growing power to walk in widening ways!

OF PRUNING AND PRODUCTION.

THE gleaming knife seems cruel, ruthless, keen,
  While throbbing flesh is shrinking from its bite,
  And darkness, like the coming of the night,
Is falling on the spirit held between
This world and that, and all things it has seen
  Flash, phantom-like, upon its failing sight.
  What words are these the pruning blade doth write
Upon the branches robbed of vivid sheen?

"*Pain means production.*" Though the wounds still
  smart,
  The bruisèd body groans against its will,
  Its ebbing life-blood soon rebounds, to fill
The mutilated limbs, and then the heart
With quickened pace takes up anew its part,
  And autumn fruits attest the gard'ner's skill.

"THE DIVINE UNREST."

If ocean rested from her ceaseless flow,
    The whole domain of Nature were unstrung;
And if man's heart should ever cease to know
    The restless striving,—of which he has sung,—
Then were his future lost at one fell blow,
    The passing bell of progress o'er him rung,
His stature stunted, then, he could not grow,
    And back to earth his useless clay were flung!

A constant longing, which he cannot quell,
    To follow where swift-footed doubt first ran;
His discontent in shady ease to dwell,
    And dogged effort to do all he can;
The aspirations words can never tell,
    All these are choicest gifts of God to man.

OF CONSCIOUSNESS.

THE ocean covers gardens wondrous fair,
   And hideous monsters, from all curious eyes,
Hides them away, save in the shallows, where
   Quite near the shore it bares its mysteries,
And yields to sight an underworld. Ah, rare
   Are days when e'en that little clearly lies
Revealed to man; and who shall ever dare
   To say, the fringe is all the sea supplies.

Deep down, below the conscious life which speaks
   Its thoughts, lie unexplorèd regions vast,
Where tangled yearnings growing sway, and cast
Entreating arms unto the light, that seeks
   To find them; but the earth-wind passing, shrieks,
   And all is tumult where his foot hath passed.

TEARS.

Spring showers are tears of childhood, soon they pass,
    And leave the sweet forget-me-nots more pure;
They freshen every tender blade of grass,
    The little griefs they quickly, surely cure.
But tears of stern maturity, alas!
    Are wild destructive torrents, hard to endure,
And gather sullenly, a leaden mass,
    With scanty power to soften, or allure.
Old age forgets the fiercer thunder rain,
As spirit cleanses off each earthly stain;
    The bliss and agony for it are past,
    An even hue o'er joy and grief are cast:
Though gentle tears of memory may fall,
The light and shade of life no more appal.

CHRISTMAS DAY.

'Tis Christmas Day! The day when joy and peace
  Were promised to a wild, tumultuous world :
  Yea, peace is planted, though she lies long furled
In human hearts ; and sure is her increase,
As sure as God ; whose hand doth never cease
  To guide the avalanche, like thunder hurled
  Upon the plain ; or tender bud close curled
Within its sheath. He shall, at last, release
His children from the prison-house of doubt,
  And set them free, in pure and perfect air
  Of love and hope ; and then each life made fair
As His who gave it, clean within, without,
Shall send from land to land a ringing shout—
  "All hail ! for men are brothers everywhere !"

THE BOILING POINT.

Go, watch a seething cauldron as it boils,
    And note the sudden stoppage of the steam;
The treacherous calmness of the surface foils
    The senses,—all is silent as a dream.
But one degree between the seeming peace
    And wildest torrents bursting all their bounds;
And, ere the raging lava currents cease,
    The shrinking air with groans and sobs resounds.
Beneath the calm, collected, courteous speech
    Which covers these tumultuous hearts of ours,
Lie surging passions which shall only reach
    To action, during strain of life's hot hours;
And yet this heat, in man and nature too,
May be the motive power great deeds to do.

REPENTANCE AND RESTITUTION.

AT the eleventh hour man may repent,—
　The thief upon the cross a pardon won,—
But can his thoughts on ease or bliss be bent,
　Until what man may do is truly done
To right old wrongs, to clear the innocent,
　To drive away the mists that hide the sun,
And close the yawning cleft his hand has rent?
　This side the grave, th' repentant man doth run
To make full restitution ; shall he lose
　Unselfishness in passing out of time,
　　And fly to sing " Hosanna," knowing well
　　The load, that for his sake, so darkly fell
On those he leaves behind ?　That were a crime
Impossible, if he have power to choose !

THE LILY.

A GENTLE maiden sings her tender song
   Of quiet joy amid her blossoms rare ;
She kisses their sweet faces, ling'ring long,
   And only plucks the fairest of the fair,
   Herself a flow'ret pure as any there.
No thought hath she of hardship or of wrong ;
   Shall any mortal in her presence dare
To flaw her girlish peace, with passion strong?

Ah no ! in sheltered gardens let her rest,
   Not hers the stormy heights of life to gain ;
   For summer sunshine and soft falling rain
Is her frail spirit fitted. Leave her, lest
   Her love awaked should bring her life-long pain,
And broken, she should wither on thy breast.

AN OPEN GRAVE.

O MOURNER, be consoled; she is not far,
  For neither earth nor sea delays the flight
  Of her ethereal essence, robed in light.
It flashes like a beam, where loved ones are;
And they who grieve too much may e'en debar
  Her entrance to the regions of the bright,
  And bring a shadow, as of earthly night,
Upon the visage that were else a star.

This world knows her no more; yet she survives!
  Awake, O hope of immortality,
And set the mourner from death's trammels free.
The narrow portal of the grave deprives
No living soul of life: that passage shrives
  The spirit from its fleshly agony.

THE PAGAN'S PROTEST.

SPEAK not to me of joy born out of tears,
　Of life transfigured in the fire of grief.
　I love the sunshine, and 'tis my belief
That happiness is best, and that it clears
The vision more completely: it endears
　All earthly life, to silver turns each leaf,
　And casts a halo round the gathered sheaf,
All nature looks her best when sun appears!

Is then this life the whole, the Christian asks?
　Is joy the end for which mankind was born?
Are there no nobler and more fruitful tasks
　Than just to glitter through a sunny morn?
Believe me, he, or she, who only basks,
　The fairest crown of life has never worn!

EXPECTATION IS PROPHECY.

IF man could see behind the aging breast,
   And read the thoughts beneath the whitened hair,
Could feel the calm exterior hardly pressed,
   By surging longings, ne'er in words laid bare,
Then would he realise that life at best
   Is not an end; it cannot still all care
Within a soul which here can find no rest,
   Yet ever hopes to find it otherwhere!

Prophetic are these aspirations; sight
   Is only possible where things exist,
     And now maturèd hearts discern a morn
To break in splendour after Time's long night.
   The mother loves her child ere she has kissed
     Its lips. E'en thus diviner life is born!

A RETROSPECT.

The end is drawing near; I seem to know
  That what I had to say is almost said;
  That one prepares to sever from my head
The lock that binds to life; that I may go
To render my account of joy and woe,
  In fairer regions of the happy dead.
  Upon my eyes a dawn begins to spread
Behind the hills of time. My lamp burns low.

Let me remember all the varied past
  In this last softened and maturèd mood.
  At first, with youth's audacity I stood
Alone, and feared not; then by grief downcast
I looked from earth, to win a hope more vast:
  I wonder, and adore; all has been good!

LOOK UPWARD.

They walked one day together, he and she,
　Along a rough field-path; a silent pair.
He inwardly repined, "There's naught to see
　Upon a road like this, that leads nowhere."
While she, with beaming eyes, looked lovingly
　At budding trees and hedgerows passing fair,
And higher yet, where on an azure sea
　The cloudlets sailed without a shadowing care.

Was that one universe these creatures saw?
　His gloomy brows were gathered to a frown,
While she forgot the beaten track worn brown,
And saw on every side a bounteous store
Of beauty, that transfigured earth's dull floor;
　For she gazed up, while he looked ever down!

OF SORROW.

I said, "This burthen is too hard to bear,
   And I will cast it from me, and go free
   To distant lands, new constellations see,
Live for myself alone, and know no care."
'Twas done; and yet sometimes the balmy air
   Took shape and weight, and laid itself on me,
   Intangible, a ghost of memory,
Rebellious hearts unwillingly must bear.

The fairest scene became a haunted spot;
   Unhurt, I stood as one bowed down with pain;
I yearned for rest, and yet she heeded not,
   For dreamless sleep I prayed,—yet prayed in vain!
And then I said, "This is the hardest lot,
   Let me go back to my own place again."

OF DISCONTENT.

If thou art satisfied with that thou hast,
　How can man teach thee aught? 'Tis seekers find
　The hidden treasures of the earth and mind;
And restless ones who ever forward cast
Their longing eyes, though outcome of the past,
　With faces to the future well inclined,
　Against the chains of custom have repined,
Undaunted by the clouds around them massed.

O man, be not content, but dredge the deep
　Within thee, till great thoughts may sail
　With safety there, nor dread a stormy gale,
But spread broad canvas to the breeze, and keep
A steady course, though roaring billows leap,
　And wailing voices warn thee thou shalt fail!

A BRIDE'S BIRTHDAY.

A CHILD I knew thee, and a fair, fresh maid;
   And now a wife art thou to whom I sing,
   And as I ponder it my heart would cling
To thee as now thou art! I tremble, am dismayed,
To think that every year, a tribute paid
   On this thy natal day, youth's knell must ring,
   That time the lines of care and age will bring;
And yet, why should I be so sore afraid,
For time, which ages thee, must age me too,
   And young together, life shall only knit
   Our hearts more closely; and the love-flame lit
Within my heart must steadier grow, more true,
For thou, O Love, hast power my life to imbue
   With earnest purpose, for thy pure soul fit.

"OUT OF THE EATER COMETH FORTH MEAT."

Upon a slough trees thrive and grow awhile,
  Seem flourishing, and deck themselves with leaves,
  But tossed by storm, no rooted strength retrieves
Th' unwonted strain; they fall in one vast pile;
Then fade, decay, become but refuse vile,
  And are absorbed into the porous soil
  To lie for centuries; until the toil
Of later days finds that which *coal* they style.
Thus e'en disaster turns to good in time;
  The ills of one age benefit the next;
  The problems which to-day have so perplexed
Sad souls, may, in some distant age or clime,
Be found the only means for ends sublime,
  Though shallow man o'er them his heart has vexed.

THE PIONEER OF PROGRESS.

"THE folly of this foolish law I see;
   Why then shall I refrain from swift advance?"
   Look back, O pioneer, with eagle glance,
And pause ere opening floodgates to a sea
Of lawlessness and fierce ferocity.
   Remember Revolution's ghastly dance,
   Then realize the force of circumstance,
And of the *outward* lives of men like thee.

A law art thou unto thyself; then stay
   Within the barrier, and ever strive
Along progressive paths to lead the way,
And train the infant future day by day.
   At no licentious liberty connive,
Yet pour on sham a penetrating ray.

REST, OR RENEWED ACTIVITY.

How shall he rest at death, whose roving feet
  The ways of life have walked without a pause,
For whom the days and years have been too fleet,
  And every season an exciting cause
  To work ? E'en night and sleep have open doors,
And problems are propounded while hearts beat
  Unconsciously; oblivion rarely pours
Her waters on the soul that finds thought sweet.

The sensuous heaven of settled, selfish peace
  Were scarcely heaven to any seeking soul ;
Its search for truth can never, never cease,
  Desiring always to explore the whole,
Its ardour and unrest can but increase
  Upon attainment of desirèd goal.

OF SINCERITY.

Sincerity bestows her silent gifts
　On open minds, as evening showers dew
　Upon the fields, refreshing them anew.
Her patient perseverance slowly lifts
The life above the superstitious drifts
　Of futile fallacies, to facts untrue,
　Restoring all distorted forms; in lieu
Of worthless dross, grains of pure gold she sifts.

She rocks the cradle of the infant truth,
　And shelters him from desecrating hands,
　Until a godlike hero bravely stands
To captivate the hearts of martial youth,
　And send them forth in regulated bands,
　Beneath his flag to conquer distant lands.

COUNT TOLSTOÏ.

FROM many lands thoughts fare on pilgrimage
   Unto the home of him who tries to rise
   Above desire of any worldly prize,
The fever-heat of avarice to assuage,
'Gainst luxury a holy war to wage,
   New pathways for the future to devise,
   Bestowing on the blind perceptive eyes,
To pierce the secret hidden 'neath his page.

A man of many sorrows, yet revered
   For honest purpose, and a heart of gold
   Most freely spent, with agonies untold,
To feed the hungry. Strange the way he steered
To gain the shore he overran, and cleared
   Of those who in the Temple bought and sold.

OF GRAVITATION.

SOME are there who perform their daily round
   Of active service, and make no complaint;
Unto the wheel of painful duty bound,
   Endure with patience, never fail or faint,
   And yet from earth contract no soiling taint,
For though the body clings to solid ground,
   The spirit gravitates, a haloed saint,
For ever upward, where its like are found.

A moment of repose, and lo, 'tis there!
   All sorrow quite forgotten, as it rings
   A rythmic measure from its rising wings;
For moving freely through the rarer air,
No shadow of perplexity or care,
   Remains to dull the rapturous song it sings.

OF SELFISHNESS.

A FROSTY fog lies on the fields and hides
   The ample sky and panorama spread
   Above, around ; and sullen thoughts are bred
In selfish hearts, restricting on all sides
The sympathies, those far-expanding guides
   By which one soul to other souls is led,
   To share with men less favoured daily bread,
In faith cast out on life's o'erflowing tides.

The fate of those condemned to icy caves,
   Where echoes shrilly answer wasted breath,
Congealing as it hangs in cloudy waves,
Is bliss compared with selfishness that laves
   In petrifying pools of living death,
Yet isolated, hates the life it craves.

A SENSITIVE PLATE.

The lightest touch pure melody creates
   On well attuned and deftly handled string,
And ah, how sensitive the mind that waits
   Reverberations of its age to sing!
No hesitation knows it, nor debates
   Of what were best to do, or say, or bring;
All sounds it hears it earnestly relates,
   And echoes on its polished surface ring.

It has been taught, perchance, as others are,
   And only moulds materials it knows,
   But far beyond that narrow limit flows,
Reflecting earth and sea, the sky and star;
   Impressions dimple on it, as it goes
Into the infinite unknown, afar.

A GOSPEL OF SCIENCE.*

GOOD news, good news, proclaimed upon the earth,
  Is sounding through the pulses of mankind,
  And if the gospel taught be true, how blind
Has been the past! Not tainted at his birth,
Not handing down fresh stains destroying worth,
  But always fitted to begin afresh,
  If but relieved from the destructive mesh
Of adverse circumstance. Of joy no dearth
Were this great message proved; then hope would raise
  Her youthful head, and look with beaming eyes
  Upon the foulest man that grovelling lies,
And sing sustaining and restoring lays
To banish dark despair from future days,
  Bestowing life as a desired prize!

* Professor Weismann's theory of the continuity of the germ-plasm.

THE ELASTICITY OF TIME.

" THE days are rigid, circumscribed and short,
   Monotonously wearisome and tame."
Not so, O sensualist; a noble aim
A widely different lesson soon had taught.
Thy days are empty rounds of pleasure, fraught
   With memories too few, and full of shame;
   But 'tis thyself, not Time, that thou shouldst blame,
Elastic he, by strong hands firmly caught;
For well-used moments draw out pliant hours
   To wonderous lengths of joy and usefulness;
   And days there are, that seem to be no less
Than infinite, so plentiful the showers
Descending on the quickly growing powers
   Of him who spends himself, his kind to bless.

NATURE'S MASQUERADE.

FAIR Nature singing, danced and played,
In summer's garb of green arrayed,
And wandered with a sober pace
Through autumn days with stately grace;
And then she longed to change her part,
To act the stoic-seeming heart.
She cast about awhile, to see
How she might do it thoroughly.
"I have been gay and grave," she said,
And now I'll feign that I am dead;
I'll clothe the world in stainless white,
And make the darkest forests light."
She chilled her breath and sent it forth
From unknown regions of the north;
Through hollow spaces of the air
Bright elfin forms, both frail and fair,
Came hovering; uncertain yet
The destination for them set.
But faster, faster, came they till
They settled down on dale and hill,
On cottage, tree, and riverside,
At first to melt and then abide.
The downy plumage of the sky
Soon buried earth from every eye,

The laden trees enchanted stood
Along the edges of the wood,
And stretched still arms across the fence,
As if deploring deadened sense,
And warding off the coming snow
Which fell above, around, below.

The world lay glitt'ring, silent, cold,
The sun stayed long behind the wold;
With crowding flakes the air grew dark,
Till earth began the gloom to mark
And changed her robes from white to grey,
Befitting dreary winter day.
Each breath hung visibly in air,
The lake assumed a face of care;
Its ruffled surface stiffened soon
To wrinkles 'neath the struggling moon.
And frowned, and tossed its tresses light,
In answer to the breath of night,
Nor smiled when eve's fair orb looked out,
But seemed to shudder or to pout.
The fettered river ceased to implore
Unheeding Nature to restore
Congealéd currents to a state
More fit with life and love to mate.

And then when snow forgot to fall,
Over the undulating pall
Of Mother Earth, long tongues of light
From glancing stars gleamed diamond bright.

No sound of beast, or song of bird,
O'er all the ghostly world was heard,
The forests and the streams were dumb,
And Nature's hour of death seemed come.
Serene and strangely still she lay,
Awaiting her last judgment day;
No requiem disturbed her rest,
No child lay sobbing on her breast;
The last of all her kind seemed she,
Unwakable eternally.

But soon the fickle dame began
To peep where once her children ran,
She wearied of her solemn game,
And then commenced to scold and blame.
The sighing breezes took her plaint
And whispered it with accents faint,
Along the frost-bound river brink,
To laden trees, and through each chink
Cracked open in the hardened ground;
Till soon two tiny shoots were found,
Which peered above the stiffened soil;
Not long the envious snow could foil
Their eager curiosity,
The whispering air above to see.
Then weary of her masquerade
Dame Nature waked each dripping glade;
And where the snowdrop hung its cup,
The hardy crocus started up,

And boldly raised her golden head
To gem once more her grassy bed.
The ice 'gan groaning on the lake,
Which rose and strained its bonds to break;
The trees shook off their tiresome load,
And gusty winds began to goad
The hedgerows, till with shrilly cry,
Unclad, they begged him pass them by.
A friendly face the sun once more
Displayed at morn, and to her core
The earth drank in reviving heat;
Her thawing pulses 'gan to beat,
Flashed messages to tree and bush,
Increased their current to a rush;
And when the nesting birds at last
Sang their sweet songs, the Masque was passed;
And Nature, glad to be alive,
Woke up all inmates of her hive,
And bade each creature rouse, and bring
Its tribute to another spring.

SEARCH IS BEST.

WHERE fringes of the ocean chafing, fret
　The wave-worn stones, a youth with eager eyes
　Is striving to discern through glowing skies,
The shore, where soon the sinking sun will set.

Upon his face fall glorious crimson rays,
　Yet is he not content to stand and look ;
　He longs to hear the words the wavelets shook
From meeting crests, ere parting diverse ways.

Some secret of the gorgeous sunset land
　They whispered, each to each in that embrace,
　And now delighted, smiling, rush and race
A happy, restless, and adventurous band.

" Shall I alone stay here and never know
　What lies beyond this beauteous, beaconing deep,
　Shall I, alive, be hushed to death-like sleep,
And o'er the ocean sailing, fail to go ?

" Ah no, I cannot stay, some shadowy hand
　Is luring me to deeds unthought before,
　Some voice is whispering a mysterious lore
To be attained, could I but understand.

SEARCH IS BEST.

"I cannot stay; my heart is beating fast
   With sudden hopes flashed on me from above,
   Their value or their emptiness to prove
I lift my anchor and forget the past."

With hasty tread he hurries to the shore
   To spread broad canvas to the summer breeze,
   And float away across unsounded seas,
Returning to his childhood's strand no more.

    .   .   .   .   .   .

Far, far away, a frail and tossing boat
   Speeds o'er the waters; though the billows roar,
   A weary man plods on with broken oar
To keep the little coble still afloat.

Its timbers strain, and threaten at each shock
   To part asunder; breezes loudly shriek,
   Tormenting words they seem to him to speak,
His parchèd lips with the salt spray they mock.

No shore in sight; clouds racing o'er the sky,
   A golden halo round the shrouded moon;
   The end is coming, coming all too soon,
And he upon the waste of waves must die.

"Give up, O man," they cry, "thy toil and rest,
   Thou sought'st the land, thy life has been in vain.
   Dost thou regret thy youth, thy long-borne pain?"
"Not so," he sighed; "I sought, and SEARCH IS BEST."

THE DYING BOY.

Sit here beside me, mother dear,
   And don't put out the light just now;
I like to see the stars appear,
   And feel your hand upon my brow.

While I lie here so quietly,
   I often see such pleasant things;
Trees wave, and birds sing merrily,
   I feel as though I rose on wings.

I quite forget I cannot walk,
   Indeed it does not matter much,
For I can always think or talk.
   Don't move your hand, I like your touch.

There's only one thing I regret,
   The time slips far too fast away.
Why, mother dear, your eyes are wet!
   Have you not had a happy day?

O there's my star; so now good-night;
   I know you're tired, because you weep,
So kiss me, and put out the light.
   He slept that night his long last sleep.

THE HEART'S REPLY.

Rippling river, tell me
What your wavelets murmur as they go :
Tell me, stay and tell me
Why they smile so gladly as they flow.

Rolling ocean, tell me
What your billows murmur to the strand ;
Tell me, sound and tell me
Why they laugh so blithely round the land.

Breezy woodlands, tell me
What your boughs are breathing to the air ;
Tell me, speak and tell me
Why they rustle gaily everywhere.

Joyous song-birds, tell me
What your swelling throats desire to say ;
Tell me, sing and tell me
Why you never weary all the day.

'Tis my heart must tell me
What the sea is saying, or the grove ;
Through it Nature tells me,
"Earth is beautiful and God is Love."

THE RULING POWER.

MEN come and go, the nations rise and fall,
While evil seems triumphant, good laid low ;
An earthquake shatters cities, and men call
For help in vain,—at least it seemeth so ;—
The arrow shot with true aim from the bow
Falls broken, though an idle schoolboy's ball
Destroys a priceless vase, and weeds will grow
Where flowers droop and die! Doth Chance rule all?

The waters move with constant ebb and flow,
And regularly day succeeds the night ;
The seeds Spring planted Autumn's hands shall mow,
And sunny noon evolves from morning light.
Yes, even now, with all the past in sight,
Man sees an ordered sequence come and go,
And Nature loses nothing of her might ;
Can fickle Chance through all things govern so ?

THE RULING POWER.

No sparrow falleth unobserved, and Chance
Can have no part in human destiny,
Though shallow, purblind man, with narrow glance,
No beautiful Necessity can see.
Plunged in a gloomy, gruesome reverie,
He sits and broods amid the whirling dance
Of long processions, which scarce seem to be
Within the sphere of Law as they advance.

Yet in the days to come, when fleeting shows
Have vanished, as the dew before the sun,
When chilling blast of earth no longer blows,
And Time's phantasmal pantomime is done,
When doubts and dreams realities have won,
And Truth's eternal sunshine melts the snows,
Then shall man see an ordered current run,
A steadfast purpose, which unaltered grows.

And standing on that summit he shall gain
A comprehensive view of the long way,
An outlook such as travellers attain
Who reach an Alpine peak at close of day;
Then looking backward, humbly shall he say,
"The plan was far too vast; I tried in vain,
With frail and finite eyes, to pierce the grey,"
So infinitely far extends the plain!

Then shall he see that paths which skirt the hills,
Which cross, and re-cross, in a network fine,
Are trending to one mount, and all the rills
To one great ocean ; and that Mind Divine
Alone can guide 'mid labyrinths that twine
Through mazy windings, to the end it wills :
The end for which all conscious souls must pine,
The triumph of pure Good o'er seeming ills.

THE VERY GATE OF HEAVEN.

Some days there are, when sky and sea and air
Are still and pure and delicately fair,
When giant mountains lie like vap'rous clouds
On the horizon, and the heat mist shrouds
Their rugged sides with veils of tender grey,
Till scarce they seem to share the light of day.
The nearer hills glow green and brown and gold,
And from the scattered houses, fold on fold
The curling smoke ascends, like incense burned
Upon an altar fire, and roofs are turned
To gleaming jewels on the brow of day,
Flashing and glitt'ring 'neath the sun's bright ray.
The wind forgets to blow, the sun to scorch,
And earth appears the hallowed, silent porch,
In which men rest a moment, ere they tread
The Holy Temple of the sainted dead.

CHANGES.

CHANGES are in the air,
  Falling softly like first flakes of the snow,
Dropping and melting there,
  Dissolved before one comes their shape to know.

Changes are in the air,
  Coming quickly o'er thought and word and deed;
Stability is rare,
  Time takes no heed of wounded hearts that bleed.

Changes are in the air,
  Fast, undefined, but wonderful and strange;
How then shall men prepare
  For that which lies beyond thought's widest range?

How doth the earth prepare
  For coming life and death to her unknown?
By earnest, constant care
  Each day to use its hours before they're flown!

A LIFE'S REVELATIONS.

BEFORE a mirror kneeling see a child,
   Who tries to fathom its mysterious deep;
   Unwinking eyes look up at her, and sleep
Flies far away: her thoughts are sad and wild.

In fascinated silence down she peers;
   "Are those the eyes of God?" she says at last,
   "Shall I into eternal flame be cast,
Because I think Him cruel? O, He hears!"

For those reflected eyes had seemed to flash!
   Unhappy child, 'tis thine own eyes grown dim,
   And thou hast thine own thoughts transferred to Him.
A teardrop falls; she starts to hear it plash.

The years roll on. A maiden wends her way
   Through flowery meads, along the fresh sea shore.
   Of God, of heaven and hell she thinks no more,
Content to live within the present day.

'Tis naught to her that tears fall bitterly,
   That she is ignorant of others woes;
   If but the sunshine follow where she goes,
She cares not where the storm-clouds chance to be.

A LIFE'S REVELATIONS.

"If God were infinite or even great,
   How soon could He put all the wrong things right.
   Can I, a feeble girl, remove the night,
Or change the world, reverse decrees of fate?

I can but laugh and love, but dance and sing,
   And feel it joyous to be thus alive;
   For pleasure only will I always strive,
And take my chance of all that life may bring."

Alas, fair girl! disease hath laid his hand
   On thy frail flesh and marred its youthful bloom;
   And o'er thy days the shadow of a tomb
Rests darkly. Rain falls fast upon the land.

She makes no moan, but day by day she thinks
   Deep thoughts that surge within unceasingly;
   Had she the choice, she now would cease to be,
And down to Death's dark portal slowly sinks.

With trembling fingers knocking, yet she fears
   To hear the warder answer that faint call;
   The groaning hinges of the gate appal
Her shrinking heart; it opes, and what appears?

Not dreary dungeons, gloomy, dank, and cold,
   But glorious gardens, bathed in sunshine bright:
   No shadows follow the celestial light,
And warmth begins her senses to enfold.

A LIFE'S REVELATIONS.

Fain would she enter in, but soon the door
   Swings back and leaves her leaning 'gainst its bolts;
   At that fresh cruelty her soul revolts,
Yet must she wend her way to earth once more.

Restored to consciousness, the light seems red
   Within the walls of the familiar room;
   And through the ever-growing, deepening gloom,
Flit floating shapes of those men call " the dead."

Ah, now she knows there is not any death,
   That life is good, that God is not unkind!
   Each day a stronger faith begins to bind
The aching body to its flick'ring breath.

Before her lies a long and thorny road,
   No strength has she to tread the toilsome way,
   And yet with courage waxing every day
She stoops to lift her heavy, cumbrous load.

Beneath its weight at first she almost sinks;
   Its form is shapeless, unaccustomed, strange;
   But unseen powers their forces round her range,
Till she no longer at the dark shape shrinks.

Then all amazed, she finds the thing she feared
   Transformed into an angel, strong to save!
   Upon his wings she smiles across the grave,
And finds the darkest spot by hope endeared.

A LIFE'S REVELATIONS.

The book of fate, so hard to understand
  In brooding childhood, and in thoughtless youth,
  Lies open, shining with transfigured truth,
Unlocked at last by Sorrow's strong right hand.

And as she reads, her heart with ardour burns
  To flow into the tide of fuller life,
  And melt to harmony discordant strife,
Till every obstacle a pathway turns.

Her hand she lays upon the heart of earth,
  That seems so still beneath its garments fair,
  And stooping low to listen, lingers there,
For 'gainst her fingers pulses spring to birth.

Below the finite lies a form divine!
  Her eyes are opened, and with glad amaze
  She sees the veil dissolve before her gaze,
As sunlight through the mist begins to shine.

OF TRIFLES.

Not a joy nor a sorrow in vain
Passes onward upon its swift way;
Each is leaving in mirth or in pain,
All unnoticed, its mark on the day.

Not a word nor a look can be lost,
Not a step ever taken alone,
Though no soul ever count up the cost,
And the path never draw forth a groan.

For the smallest of waves sets afloat
Many motions which vibrate afar;
And a trill from a nightingale's throat
May be felt,—it is said,—in a star.

How appalling if such be the fact,
For we all are so careless in speech;
And so reckless in many an act,
And so thoughtless, yes, e'en when we teach.

FULFILLED, YET UNFULFILLED.

(A TALE OF SECOND-SIGHT.)

Upon the broad white doorstep of her home,
Erect, an agèd Highland woman stood,
And watched the road by which all travellers come
Bound Northward, past the waving pine tree wood.
Her eyes grew absent as her thoughts roamed South,
Unto the son away in distant lands ;
Her paling cheek, the quiver round her mouth,
Spoke volumes of distress, like those hard hands
With their tight grasp upon her apron-strings.
Those near her stood in silent sympathy,
They saw her mind was wandering forth to things,
To distant scenes, her neighbours could not see.

" He comes," she said at length, with fixèd eyes,
" He comes across the deep,—I see him now,—
And now I lose him." Eagerly she tries
To follow a ship's course with knitted brow.
Fear, anger, agony, passed like the shades
Of fleeting clouds across her dream-rapt face ;

FULFILLED, YET UNFULFILLED.

"There, there he is! I see the dripping blades
Of oars, among the rowers is his place."
A moment's silence, then again, "He seems
Distressed, disfigured,—and ah, worse,—disgraced!"
And with a cry she turned from the full beams
Of midday sun; her way she blindly traced
To her accustomed place beside the fire,
Not one dared then intrude upon her grief.
Alone she lived thenceforth, nor seemed to tire,
Nor gave herself a moment of relief.

Weeks lengthened into months, months to a year,
And summer once again had clothed the land;
A feeble cry of weakness or of fear
Fell on her startled ears, and stilled her hand.
"The dreaded day has come at last," she said,
"Disgraced, degraded, he comes back to me;"
And as she spoke, her face glowed dusky red
With bitter shame and utter misery.
Then opening wide the door, upon the stone
Where she had stood, foreseen, a year ago,
A rag-clothed figure lay. With stifled moan
She murmured, "Yes, I knew it would be so."
She stooped and lifted that poor wasted lad
In her strong arms as though he were a child.
"Mother, I am come home,— to die,— 'tis sad,
But not the worst," he said, and ah, he smiled!
Then hope awoke within her burthened breast,
She laid him gently in his father's place;

"Thou hadst been, mother, far, far more distressed
Had I brought riches,—and with them disgrace!"
"My lad, my bairn," she cried, "my own good son,
How hast thou eased me of my sharpest pain!
And death is naught, for soon my work all done,
I know that we shall meet in Heaven again."

OF CHOICE.

In deep recesses of the human heart
    The battlefields of life are daily fought;
For here and now the ways of Being part,
    And man decides the struggle in his thought.

Momentous questions each soul must decide,
    Eternal issues on its answers rest.
The scoffing tongue and scornful eye deride
    The truth, yet must endure its searching test.

Sometimes unconsciously men make their choice,
    They drift into decision—ah, sad state!—
The limbo of the neutral; and what voice
    Shall wake them to abhor the idler's fate?

No angry Deity debars the base
    From entrance to the Heaven of the pure.
The sluggard cannot, *cannot* win the race;
    Himself his judge, inevitably sure.

O that some angel with his clarion voice
    Would rouse the nations from their foolish hope
Vicariously to save themselves. 'Tis choice,
    And choice alone, decides life's future scope.

THE HARVEST MOON.

How redly through the mists of earth
Thou risest to thy harvest birth,
To bring hard toil and banish dearth
    From men away;
Thou messenger of work and mirth
    And gath'rings gay.

The dew is falling all around,
On every leaf and blade is found,
Yet not the faintest patt'ring sound
    Disturbs the sense;
And over all the level ground
    The fog is dense.

The full ripe ears of golden wheat
Are bending 'neath the dew's soft beat,
And here and there late songsters greet
    Thy friendly face,
Where gurgling rivers swiftly meet
    In close embrace.

THE HARVEST MOON.

The cooing pigeon of the wood,
Hath ceased awhile to seek his food
In those broad fields where leaning stood
    The early sheaves,
And nestles in a restful mood,
    Beneath the leaves.

The lowing kine are still at last,
And their broad shadows, darkly cast
Across the meadows, seem more vast
    Than e'er at morn.
And timid travellers' hearts beat fast,
    By fear are torn.

On heathy hills and down the dale,
Through balmy breeze or stormy gale,
Thou gazest on the varied tale
    Of human life;
Thou hearest the sad heart's wild wail
    Of doubt and strife.

Across the sea thy soft beams shine,
And lay a pathway o'er the brine,
To link the earthly and divine,
    That side to this,
Till here and there alike are thine,
    And full of bliss.

And happy lovers, pacing late
Beside the well-known trysting-gate,
Through light and shadow softly prate
    Of love and hope;
Then hand in hand they meditate
    On life's wide scope.

And ere they part, thy radiance brings
To them upon its silvery wings,
A vision of diviner things
    Which they may share.
And list! the curfew's call-note rings
    Upon the air.

Fair orb! if I could rise as thou
Art rising o'er my head just now,
And with thy light upon my brow
    Look down below,
I dared not live as I live now,
    And judge men so!

No cloudy wreath obscures thy light,
Above the steaming earth's dark night
Thou shinest, waxing still more bright,
    And yet too soon
Thou yieldest to the morning's might,
    O Harvest Moon!

THE REALM OF MUSIC.

In music lies a Fairy-land,
   A timeless, shoreless place;
Beneath ethereal, fadeless trees
   Thoughts airy circles trace.

Elves play therein mysterious pranks,
   And groping goblins live,
Sad changelings sigh for human love,
   Which fairies cannot give.

Bright fancies dance with soundless tread,
   And hopes have no fixed size;
While e'en th' invisible is seen,
   And pleasure is surprise!

Waves surge and break in melody,
   And cascades fall with song,
The hills and dales can speak aloud,
   Voices to them belong.

And all are welcome there whose souls
   Nurse wishes to fulfil.
This Fairy-land has always been,
   And is existing still.

MY RING.

Within the plain gold ring I wear
    My story I can read:
A few poor words are graven there,
    Yet they are all I need.

Above the words a vacant space
    Tells of a childhood gay,
Of all the hopes and dreams which grace
    A maiden's joyous way.

" June 4th of eighteen eighty-eight,"
    That is not much to say,
But my whole future is the freight
    Of that eventful day.

And now I add a few words more—
    Thy birthday, boy, that's all!
A date which means new joys in store,
    Or griefs,—which shall befall?

Beneath these lines another space,
    Untouched by graver's art.
Who knows the story which that place
    Shall write upon my heart?

A DAY-DREAM.

A MAIDEN stood beside a purling brook,
And at her feet its rippling tresses shook;
Her heart awaking from its childish sleep,
With trembling ecstasy began to leap.
The birds were calling, calling, o'er the stream,
And myriad insects danced upon the beam
Which fell across her path along the grass.
"O river," sang she, "thou dost ever pass
To bring fresh water ere the old is gone;
And yet I love thee, though thou flowest on.
Would I might follow this new wave I see
Dash down the mountain side so merrily."

Her eyes grew dreamy, steady, dark, and still;
Her feet seemed drawn along against her will,
Now swiftly, and now slowly, as the wave
The signal, by its rushing, staying gave;
Until a booming sound fell on her ears,
And then a treacherous calmness roused her fears.
Constrained to follow, where great boulders stood
In an aggressive and defiant mood,
Dividing the broad stream, which parting, roared,
And gasping, down a rocky slope was poured,

To leap at last into a great abyss,
The maiden heard the water's angry hiss,
And saw its eddies swirl between the walls
Of rugged stone, through which perforce it falls.

The dashing spray obscured awhile her sight,
But through the dark ravine soon shone a light;
And thither ran the water with a rush,
Regardless of the briar, tree, or bush.
She followed still with throbbing, aching heart,
Her feet on those sharp rocks began to smart;
An opening gained, the sun shone through, to pour
His warmth upon her shivering flesh once more.
This danger past, she kept her way with ease,
Until again the birds called from the trees
Familiar notes that forced her tears to flow,
For always onward, onward, must she go.

The water soon forgot its dreadful haste,
And lingered lovingly along the waste
Of moorland, list'ning to the plover's note,
And toying with the burnished trout which float
And dart and flash from stone to stone, then leap
To glitter in the sunshine, and plunge deep
Into the sullen pools that here and there,
Their inky garments in weird silence wear.
The moorland left at last, far, far behind,
Through well-tilled fields the growing stream must
     find

A widening pathway, fed on every side
By runlets, added to the swelling tide.
Serenely quiet then its stately pace,
Until the mill-dam reached, it swerved to race
Along a narrow channel, there to turn
A mighty wheel.
     Among the springing fern
The maiden waited to observe its task,
And fain had rested there, but dared not ask,
For onward, ever onward, like a fate,
The river ran, and would not pause or wait.
Past verdant lawns and stately mansions tall,
Past forest edges and a graveyard wall,
Past scattered houses, hamlets, a small town,
And under bridges whose dark shadows frown,
All day she wandered; till the evening shade
Began to deepen, into night to fade.
And then great, glaring eyes gleamed through the dark,
And belching chimneys threw their fiery mark
Across the vault of ever-darkening hue,
And stars came trembling one by one to view.
Vast, shapeless boats, with lights on each dull prow,
Passed phantom-like, and furrowed the stream's brow.
She stood at length upon a massy quay,
And ah, what awful sights were there to see!
Down narrow lanes came foul, debauchèd reek,
"Can these be WOMEN who in curses speak?

And children these," she thought, "who scream and
    fight,
Regardless of the darkness of the night?"

She lingered there. A stirring at her heart
Seemed bidding her to stay and do her part
In the redemption of the world from sin ;
But from the river rose a startling din,
The signal-horns of vessels on its breast ;
And oh, the river would not, could not rest !
Past factories and gaunt, bare ribs of ships,
It glided, glided, till from moaning lips
An accent new seemed on the air to float,
So faint, its presence she could scarcely note ;
But soon the river in uneven waves
Chattered its teeth and groaned as through dark
    caves ;
The light buoys danced upon the broken sheen
Of that rough surface, and the stars were seen
Serene and still above, but there below
Tossed up and down, in constant ebb and flow.
The river halted,—seemed e'en to turn back,
And straining ship ropes caught its floating wrack.

She stood amazed to see where she had come !
She called unto the river ; he was dumb :
But other voices sounded from the strand,
First far away, and then quite near at hand ;

A salty breath lay moist upon her face,
And very solemn seemed the meeting place,
Where messengers from earth's fair scenes first greet
The ocean waves, as they so wildly beat
Against the rocky walls which bound the land,
Embrace, and ebb together, hand in hand.

The maiden sobbed, "Is this the end of pain,
Have I come here, so far, and come in vain?
Are rivers lost when once they reach the sea?
If so, 'twere better, better not to be!"

"Be still, wild heart," the ocean seemed to say,
" I take this mountain water far away;
No longer fresh and shallow as of yore,
But deep and strong it beats a farther shore.
It carries in its heart the sacred past
Unchangeable, which must for ever last,
And joyfully flows out to learn once more
The secrets which the Future keeps in store."

THE SISTERS.

Two children kneel at eventide,
    "Our Father," trustfully to say;
The mother with a tender pride
    Still lingers near to hear them pray.

Two maidens at God's altar stand
    To take for life a solemn vow:
This goes henceforth with ring on hand,
    And that with bandage on her brow.

Two women at an open grave
    Regret a mother's shortened life;
Then each to each her blessing gave,
    The saintly maid and happy wife.

Two shining forms at Heaven-gate
    Are sore amazed once more to meet.
In silence, hand in hand, they wait
    For words of welcome, strong and sweet.

The guardian of the blest espies
    The sisters as, with awe-struck hearts,
They enter there: his gentle eyes
    Look kindly, and all fear departs.

Then thrilling voices on their ears,
    Like sound of many waters, swell;
And soon the angel-mother steers
    Her course to those she loved so well.

She leads them both with gentle force,
    Before the Heavenly Father's seat.
God knows no better, and no worse,
    In those two women at His feet.

"Ye faithful, welcome! ye have won
    The victory in earth's long strife;
Rest now awhile; what ye have done
    Hath paved the way to fuller life.

"One talent ye have kept so bright,
    That ten shall soon become your care.
Enter, O children, into light,
    And work once more in this pure air."

A DAY IN JUNE.

A DAY IN JUNE.

(BAMBOROUGH.)

A JOY it is to-day to live and look
Upon this perfect page of Nature's book:
The faintest haze of heat lies o'er the fields,
Afar the smith his mighty hammer wields,
And that sharp ring of iron struck with skill,
The air with its grand note of toil doth fill.
Some happy children play upon the walls
Of th' ancient Castle, which no more appals
The stranger as he nears its massy keep;
No clouds of war around its casements creep,
But gentle Charity, the gift of God,
Hath her abode where mailèd men once trod.
The grassy links are whispering to the breeze,
A few white gulls are floating o'er the seas;
The shining crescent of an ample bay
From point to point absorbs the sun's bright ray,
And where the ebbing tide leaves margins bright,
The fleecy clouds reflect their vaporous light.
The roseate tern calls loudly from an isle,
Upon which wavelets wash with winning smile;
A lighthouse lifts its lantern to the sky,
And round its summit the wild sea-birds fly;

No need to-day for its revolving glare,
The sea its calmest, purest garb doth wear.
A day of days this daughter fair of June,
Whose evening shadows deepen all too soon;
Yet where she smiled, each restless heart hath found
Its sorrow sanctified, and its joy crowned.

THE PROGRESS OF LIBERTY.

The strain at first falls faintly on the ear,
    Through long dark vistas of the storied past;
And one by one the stars of hope appear,
    Their feeble rays upon the night to cast.

The secret whispered tremblingly in fear,
    Mooted in terror of the powers that be,
Gathers disciples from lands far and near,
    And swells into a song of Liberty!

The leader with his strong, prophetic voice,
    Thunders his warnings at both priest and king:
Draws thousands after him, who know no choice,
    But do his will, and learn his songs to sing.

The reckless, thoughtless, to the standard flock.
    Disturb the solemn tread of marching feet:
On sacred ground tumultuous dances rock
    With a resistless, ceaseless, rhythmic beat.

The banner floating gaily on the breeze,
    Attracts the idlers from the peopled plain;
The earnest soldier heeds them not, he sees
    The snow-capped summit which he hopes to gain.

THE PROGRESS OF LIBERTY.

The toil increases, careless followers turn
    Unto the sheltered pastures whence they came;
The resolute battalions now must earn
    Success and praise, or failure and foul blame.

The ranks are thinning fast; for pain and death
    Run riot 'mid that sacrificing band;
But each cheers on with his last failing breath
    The others, saying, "Triumph is at hand!"

So onward still, and upward, through the dark
    They toil beneath the pitying, waning stars;
Until along the mountain-line they mark
    The blackness breaking into streaks and bars.

'Tis won at last! Upon a dizzy height
    The way-worn wanderers cry, "O Victory!"
For in the distant East they see a light,
    The dawning of a world-wide Liberty!

ESCAPED!

(SONG.)

I LAY my dearest in the grave,
   And tears dim strangers' eyes.
They say thou'rt dead! They surely rave—
   Pure goodness never dies.

The earthly falls to earth again;
   But thou wert not of clay.
Thy body, racked and rent with pain,
   Hath let *thee* slip away.

The outward form lies there, 'tis true,
   But thou art living yet!
I deck thy grave with flowers, not rue,
   No tear my eyes shall wet.

DREAMS.

We dream and then we do, to dream once more;
  We think, and from the thought the deed proceeds;
  And ere the world was formed, some mind must needs
Have pictured Chaos ceasing from her roar.

The dreamer, once reviled, becomes at length
  The prophet of a later, wiser age,
  And every dreamer turning a new page,
Is adding to the truth a store of strength.

To-morrow with its acts is lying furled
  In floating visions of the present day;
  Fruition gained, new aspirations play,
And to a fancied future thought is whirled.

For fancy is far larger than the fact;
  No kiss is half so sweet upon the lip,
  No pain so bitter in its fiercest grip,
As when despair or hope were free to act.

The yearning heart, the patient, toiling brain,
   In love no man can touch, finds purest joy,
   In knowledge none can see, a life's employ.
Why love or think, save some dreamed end to gain?

Man were not man without these beaconing gleams
   Of earth transfigured, or of Heaven near.
   The prisoned soul were dead and buried here,
Save for these unsubstantial, fleeting dreams.

THE SEARCH FOR TRUTH.

I.

We grasp at shadows in our early youth,
And call the phantoms perfect, full-orbed Truth.
We comprehend,—we say,—its rounded whole,
All that there is in earth or sky or soul;
But as warm breath disturbs the chilly air
The frost flowers fade; nor can our utmost care
Rebuild them on the window where but now
They seemed so solid: then in rage we vow
That naught eternal is, naught worth the search,
We cling, we mortals, to a narrow perch
Above a great abyss where Chaos dwells.
A sob of bitter disappointment tells
Of hopes extinguished, dreams quenched in despair,
And then contemptuously we 'gin prepare
Short life to spend on pleasure's giddy round,
To be at last upon its treadmill found.

THE SEARCH FOR TRUTH.

II.

MATURED, we laugh at those first, foolish dreams,
The Truth,—we say,—comes but in broken gleams;
The world were very poor and mean indeed
If all it held were semblance of a weed.
For now we see that far beyond the home,
Beyond the earth and sky's o'er-arching dome,
Stretch out infinities of space, and world
On world is 'fore our wondering eyes unfurled.
So much there is to know, then let us keep
In this enclosure where we eat and sleep;
Here be content, that we may never stray
Into the wilderness to lose our way.
The fields are wide, their beaten tracks are fair,
The hedges high and balmy too the air,
Let others,—if they will,—explore the sea
And plumb the depths of Truth's infinity.

THE SEARCH FOR TRUTH.

III.

WE sow and reap, and garner in our store
Of that we chose, and then we sigh for more;
Chill winter comes with furrowed brow of care,
And storm-stripped, swaying arms all gaunt and bare;
He rudely rends the wall of quickset hedge,
And lo! on every towering mountain-ledge
Lie lines of freshly fallen, glistening snow,
While bitter breezes swiftly come and go
Across the pastures, and a frosty rime
Falls on loved heads beneath the touch of time,
Till one by one they shrivel and decay,
And life runs slowly into death away.
Unsheltered now, and standing all alone,
Contentment gone, the soul begins to moan
That joy and beauty have a reign so short,
That Truth through summer days has not been sought.

THE SEARCH FOR TRUTH.

IV.

THE bounds of Time are passed, but Space remains
To bind the Soul in her enormous chains;
Once more aspiring it fares forth in quest
Of Truth's completed circle, nor can rest.
With wheeling flight and ever greater speed
It cleaves its way. Soon now,—it says,—indeed
That end to this will join, and I shall see
Fair Truth in her august entirety.
But ah! the meeting ends spring far apart,
And upward, onward, must th' amazed soul start!
At last it learns one wondrous fact and true,
On which hang issues vast and not a few;
It looks above, below, beyond, around,
And not a trace of any end is found!
No ORB is TRUTH, perfect, compact, complete,
But SPIRAL, springing up fresh heights to greet!

THE SEARCH FOR TRUTH.

V.

DISMAYED, the panting soul is flung aloft,
Time's hour-glass gone, now Space her robe has doffed!
No Time, no Space, no boundaries are left,
The spirit of its cherished aim bereft
To see the whole of that it saw in part,
Poised quiv'ring, fears and quakes afresh to start.
It almost longs that it had never been,
So infinite the vista it has seen!
Sweet Hope of plumage is divested too,
How shall her feeble wings their strength renew,
To bring the failing courage fresh rebound?
Ah, list! on undulating waves of sound
A soft yet piercing voice thrills through the air,
" Upward and onward, Truth lies ever THERE."

THE AGED FISHERWOMAN.

("BESIDE THE SEA.")

Nay, I am never lonely here,
    The waves are always company;
And though I sometimes shed a tear,
    I'm happiest beside the sea.

Well yes, I'm old, the cliffs are steep,
    That's just as true as true can be;
But then I know I could not sleep
    Without the hushing of the sea.

And why I love the sea so much?
    It's everything, my dear, to me,
The only thing death cannot touch;
    I've always lived beside the sea.

When I was quite a little child,
    I used to play about that quay;
And there, where those great stones are piled,
    I met my husband, home from sea.

I often wake at night and hear
   Him calling lustily to me,
"All safe, my lass." Why should I fear?
   He always called so from the sea.

The ocean cruel, do you say?
   Ah well, I'm used to it, you see;
And I'll stay by it, if I may,
   I want to die beside the sea!

AN AUTUMN MORNING.

A SOFT grey mist lies on the distant hills,
A heavy line of fog the valley fills;
The luscious grass is bending 'neath the dew,
And jewelled silver webs exposed to view
Extend from blade to blade, from flower to flower,
Then through the dimness of the morning hour,
The cottage homes send up their curling wreaths
Of thin blue smoke, to drift where bending sheaves
Shake off the pearly drops from hanging ears,
And lo! above the pines the sun appears
To wake deep blushes on each mountain side,
And throw the gates of morning open wide.
The whirr of reaping steals upon the air,
A few late songsters twitter here and there,
Till from the west a balmy zephyr springs
To bring full day upon its whispering wings.

NOT FALLEN, BUT EVOLVING.

No, ours is not a fallen state
From which we slowly rise again;
'Twas growing mind did first create
Fair Paradise undimmed by pain.
From lowliest forms of life and thought
Has man evolved to that he is,
By labour has each stage been bought,
And conquest of dark mysteries.

At first man roamed unclad and wild,
Yielded to passion like the beasts,
Had not the knowledge of a child,
And gorged himself at his rude feasts.
Then thousands died of want and cold,
And maidens lived a slavish life,
Fierce men were cruel to the old,
And superstitious fear was rife.

The savage knew not tenderness,
But hunted, fished, then ate and slept,
No other's wrongs would he redress,
But stealthily for vengeance crept.
Unnumbered ages thus he roamed,
And learned a little here and there,
Until in cups the fruit juice foamed,
And fire subdued the chilly air.

From families evolved the tribe
Through swiftly passing centuries,
And tribal safety was the bribe
By which man learned his kind to please.
So ever toward a higher plane
Civilisation worked its way,
Till each strove less for selfish gain,
And sympathy began to play.

As brother, then as husband, friend,
He lived and worked for other lives;
And tribal customs upward tend,
The State, with equal laws arrives.
Not history, but prophecy,
Is perfect peace and innocence,
Man climbing up unceasingly,
Not sliding into decadence.

We know to what he has attained,
How quickly he is rising still,
Compared with the slow progress gained
In ages past; but not until
The State is merged in world-wide bond
Of Brotherhood and mutual love,
Shall Eden's glades and groves be found,
The types of heaven, man's home above.

TWILIGHT THOUGHTS.

Through many shadows with unfaltering feet
    I walked as evening fell,
And watched the fragrant blossoms fade and fleet
    That I had loved so well;
Recalling bygone days when inward calm
Distilled its healing dew, and shed its balm
    On painful hours,
While friendly faces hovered near, to greet
    The failing powers,
With sweet assurances that naught can harm
    A life like ours.

The saddened soul sent forth no moan, resigned
    To bear its heavy cross;
At faded joys not once the heart repined,
    Endured each crowding loss
With quiet strength sent down to direst need;
Fresh thoughts formed pathways for a spirit freed
    From every worldly care,
That subtile rapture it might surely find
    In clearer, purer air.

But ah, that gift of peace
Has fled from active days of strenuous toil,
And dreary sounds increase
Around the trodden way, my steps to foil,
For when I would do well,
Such threatening billows swell,
That hope, dismayed, dares not her wings to try,
And aspiration withers to a sigh.
Where gentle accents fell
The feverish lips cry out in agony.

Dost Thou, O God, judge men by what they *are*,
Or by the deep *desire*
That finds no outlet through the cramping bar
Of adverse circumstance, too strong by far
For weaklings who aspire
To bear a holy fire
Within the breast, consuming lower things.
Dull embers kindle not, and failure stings
To wailings of desire.

Desire to leave this ceaseless round of strife,
And lie in childlike rest
On some serener breast ;
To feel a soothing stillness steal through life,
Till quiet comes to cure

The passion and the petulance so rife,
    With accents strong and sure,
Upon the heart indelibly impressed,
That it may suffer action's searching test,
    Yet to the end endure!

    O soul, be of good cheer,
Look back upon the path thy feet have trod,
    And cease, weak heart, to fear
The stinging of the purifying rod.
    Thou hast borne agony,
    Bear now activity,
And though the goal be hidden from thy sight,
The lamp of duty shall illume the night.
    A Father leadeth thee
Unto the dawning of Eternal Light.

WHENCE?

WHENCE come these fancies flocking through the mind,
　Trooping and thronging faster every day;
And whence the glamour glittering to blind
　Glad eyes to effort on the chosen way?

Whence come these memories that dimly rise
　Through daily duties of an active life;
And whence the shrinking, lingering to apprise
　Sad souls that evil influence is rife?

Whence comes this sudden peace when all seems dark,
　Steadfast within when grief is at its worst;
And whence comes hope that like a hidden spark,
　Relights the embers, dull and cold at first?

Whence comes this life we feel but never see,
　Which permeates creation to its verge;
And whence the soul that ever longs to be
　Far from the shore where Time's rough shallows surge?

A CHRISTMAS STORY.

'Twas Christmas Eve, a filmy veil of snow
    Lay o'er the fields, on every hilly ledge;
The air was still, yet ever seemed to go
    In sighs along the whitened river edge.

The stars were shining brightly overhead,
    But all the east was draped in sullen grey;
More snow was coming, and my path still led
    O'er hill and dale, a lonely, dreary way.

Ere long, upon a sheltered plateau near,
    An old and straggling farmhouse I espied,
And soon determined thitherward to steer;
    'Twere strange, I thought, if shelter were denied.

For up these dales beat hospitable hearts
    In which suspicion finds the smallest place;
I loved to rove in unfrequented parts,
    And study every quaint, determined face.

To rest awhile beside the fire I asked,
    And was invited in most heartily,
Then all the house contained was quickly tasked
    To make a truly welcome guest of me.

A CHRISTMAS STORY.

The kitchen glowed in ruddy, leaping flame,
    The dogs looked up with doubtful, watchful gaze,
But patting them the farmer spoke each name,
    And stirred the fire afresh to make a blaze.

A mighty cheese soon stood upon the board,
    With cakes and ale, old-fashioned Christmas cheer;
My plate was by my host most amply stored,
    And then he said, "To-night you'd best stay here.

"It looks as if 'twould be a heavy fall,
    And you might lose your way up these wild dales;
You're very welcome, sir, to one and all,
    We're rough, but farmhouse ration rarely fails."

We lit our pipes, and smoking chatted long
    Of places and the people round about;
In this man's life that something had gone wrong
    I knew without the shadow of a doubt.

"You wonder," said he, "we're so quiet here
    O' Christmas Eve." I felt he wished to talk;
And then I saw slip down a furtive tear,
    Though he arose across the floor to walk.

He looked outside, then settled down again;
    "It was my wedding-day to-day," he said,
"And somehow marriage brought her naught but pain,
    She was a frail, wee, town-bred lass I wed.

"It's lonely here no doubt for town-bred folk,
　　But she was brave enough and settled down."
His hands were clasped and trembling as he spoke,
　　To stop the tears he almost seemed to frown.

"Ten years ago it was I brought her home,
　　And she seemed failing like a longish while;
But when the little lad was born, she came
　　To like the place; 'twas nice to see her smile.

"She loved that bairn o' hers with all her heart,
　　And couldn't bear him ever out of sight;
But I made up my mind the two must part
　　To let her have her proper sleep at night.

"Why how I talk! to make the story short,
　　It's just three years ago this very Eve
We lost him; every place around was sought
　　Both far and near, as you may well believe.

"It was a wild and bitter night, but still
　　The Waits had managed t' get as far as here;
They couldn't struggle further up the hill,
　　But stayed and sang a bit, in hope 'twould clear.

"But 'stead of that it got far worse, and they
　　Set off quite late to make their homeward road.
I think I never saw the sky so grey,
　　The air was loaded, and all night it snowed.

A CHRISTMAS STORY.

Said I to th' wife, 'It's late, so don't you go
    Disturbing little Robbie in his sleep.'
She didn't like the order, that I know,
    And when I think of it, I can't but weep.

"I scarce can tell you, sir, how we all felt
    When Christmas morning came; for do you see
If I'd not stopped her, she'd have gone and knelt
    To kiss him in his little bed. Ah me!

"Well, he was gone, and all that e'er we could,
    Was done to find him; need I tell you that?
We searched the sheds and garden, yards and wood;
    My conscience gnawed me like a half-starved rat.

"For though poor Alice never once complained,
    I had been hard with her, sometimes unkind
About the lad; her awful silence pained
    Me worse than any scolding could, I mind.

"One night she'd been asleep a bit, I think,
    Sitting just over there beside the fire,
And jumped up with a cry that made me shrink;
    The veins upon her brow stood out like wire.

"'I see him lying 'neath a heap of snow'
    She sobbed at last, 'and all around is dark;
It seems to me a place I ought to know,
    Yet nothing can I see the spot to mark.

"'It looks to me just like a great square grave,
   It's standing all alone, and seems quite high.'
Of course, I fancied she'd begun to rave,
   And if we didn't find the boy, she'd die.

"'Twas getting on by that to New Year's night,
   And every day snow fell, and great drifts grew;
About the bairn we got no hint of light,
   And that he must be dead by then, I knew.

"My wife, poor thing, she wandered round the place,
   And never seemed to sit a moment still;
I can't forget her pale and wretched face,
   It haunts me, sir; I think it always will.

"I'm hard enough at bearing most of pain,
   But that was like a fire within my breast.
I would not live that dreadful week again
   For all the world. She couldn't, couldn't rest.

"Well, I was working late out in the fold
   On New Year's night; and there rose such a shriek!
The very thought on't turns me deadly cold,
   She'd found him, sir, and hadn't power to speak.

"Her dream had lingered always in her mind,
   And she had grown quite sure that he was near;
And there, in pulling up a spare room blind
   The very heap she'd seen lay 'fore her clear.

A CHRISTMAS STORY.

" 'Twas just outside a sort of long glass door,
    His fav'rite place in summer time for play,
His rabbits lived there when 'twas warm, and store
    Of flowers in pots he liked, to make it gay.

" 'Twas over a bit glass place I had built
    For Alice; she'd a love for pretty things,
And working there she often used to lilt
    The bonnie songs a gentle lassie sings.

"Although it's high, we knew 'twas safe enough,
    It's railed all round, the laddie too was short;
Besides, he wasn't one was ever rough,
    He was your pretty, clinging, quiet sort.

"And there she'd found him nestled closely in
    Beside the empty hutches; and the snow
On such a place is never very thin;
    It gathers there, and doesn't easy go.

"You wonder may-be none of us should hear
    The lad, who must have cried, that's very sure;
You must remember all of us were here
    With th' Waits. Ah, after-thinking doesn't cure!

" It's not the sort of house a man would choose;
    It's rambling, and a bairn might scream his last
At yon far side, and it would be no use,
    With all these doors and windows shut, and fast.

"His mother she lived on until the wall
    Behind his death-place blossomed out again;
And then she joined him; it would e'en appal
    A stranger if I told him all her pain.

"The folk around keep saying, 'Take a wife
    To make the place a bit more cheery-like.'
But no; I mean to work while I have life,
    But new roots in this world I'll never strike.

"There's nothing that could bring forgetfulness,
    And faults like mine are best to live alone;
For I was cruel to her, nothing less;
    You cannot make a pearl out of a stone.

"I couldn't bear to hear a loud-voiced wench;
    And I'm by far too coarse for such as she,
—Alice, I mean,—and it would be a wrench
    To see her pretty things touched carelessly."

The fitful firelight flickered round and round
    The rugged farmer's bowed and grizzled head;
It seemed to me a holy halo bound
    By sorrow, in remembrance of the dead.

"What tragedy, presented on the boards,
    Was ever half so sad," I thought, "as this?
Each haunting memory the strong man hoards,
    As lovers treasure up a loved one's kiss."

He thought himself unworthy, hard and cold,
  And yet 'twere hard to find a heart so true.
Such love as his is neither bought, nor sold,
  To gain it is a conquest known to few.

His loneliness had left him too much time
  To brood o'er all the sad, unchanging past;
But steadfast hearts like that have depths sublime,
  Which must be something great, or good, at last.

LORD ARMSTRONG.

True son of the strong, patient North, thy name
Is noised abroad with an unsullied fame;
Upon thy native place 'tis graven deep
Where glowing furnace fires their night-watch keep;
In rugged characters of constant toil
'Tis written large; but on the grateful soil,
In finest tracery of verdant green
To many eyes it is more plainly seen,
For at thy word the waste a garden grows,
Forgets the briar to bring forth the rose;
And frowning hills, erst desolate and bare,
A garment now of fairest foliage wear.
With generous hand thou fill'st the furrows full,
That other lives a harvest fair may cull.
In thee a steady fire of genius burns,
Translating into practice all it learns;
In arts of war, and peace, art thou renowned,
And with the love of thousands thou art crowned;
While there are many more who know thee not,
Who yet should thank thee that their sordid lot
Is sweeter grown; set free from squalid streets,
They roam at will, where Art with Nature meets.

Their happy faces, bright with glad amaze,
Are all unconsciously thy truest praise.
That help is thine, which only upward lifts;
Thy gains have fruited into princely gifts.
Apart from faction and from party strife,
Thou liv'st thine own consistent, noble life.

PICTURES OF A LIFE.

A SPORTIVE child with eyes of azure hue,
   With merry laugh and feet that never tire,
To whom a narrow street is a wide view,
   A string upon two reeds an angel's lyre;
   The glowing heart of its own nursery fire
A fairy-land, which strangely doth renew
   Each day its wondrous cave and magic spire.
O happy girl, was ever life like you?

A maiden now with flowing, shining hair
   And smiling lips, looks out beneath her hand;
She sees a glorious daylight dawning where
   In giant undulations mountains stand.
   And ah! she yearns to join the white-winged band
That cleaves its way to yonder rarer air;
   For here and now fulfil not her demand,
"Give me," she says, " life's glittering crown to wear."

A woman weeps upon a wave-washed shore,
   Her pale lips pressed together, straight with pain:
The mighty ocean, with a threatening roar,
   Breaks at her feet. She gazes o'er the main,

Determined still her distant goal to gain.
"On this side, O my God, naught can restore
   My failing strength; here have I toiled in vain.
Is this the end? An answer I implore."

A silent form upon a narrow bed,
   With closèd eyes and raiment purest white;
Her work all done, her burning words all said,
   She rests at last. One taper's glimmering light
   Illumes the yawning blackness of the night,
And weaves a golden halo round her head.
   Ah! what is this that breaks upon her sight?
A vision of new life; and she has fled!

SNOW IN SPRING.

The Snow is falling, falling,
And dense grey clouds obscure the risen sun;
   While birds are calling, calling,
"Too soon, too soon our building was begun."

   The hills are fleeting, fleeting
Away from sight, though yesterday so clear;
   And lambs are bleating, bleating,
Though nestling to the anxious mother near.

   The earth is sighing, sighing
For that embrace in which so late it lay:
   Frail blossoms dying, dying,
Regret the brevity of beauty's day.

   The day is waning, waning,
And the blue hill-tops kiss not the blue of sky;
   Deep dales are plaining, plaining,
With muffled wail and soft, distressful cry.

   But see; a gleaming, gleaming,
As sunshine struggles faintly through its shroud;
   And soon Spring beaming, beaming
With happy smiles, forgets the passing cloud.

"OUT OF MUCH TRIBULATION."

DISTRESSING disappointments fall too fast
   Upon the heart bowed down with weight of care,
And load on load upon the soul is cast
   Which hoped to find its lot so free and fair.

This plan destroyed, and that scourged with fierce scorn,
   Misunderstood and standing all alone,
With furrowed brow and heart with anguish torn,
   The frail tongue plains its unavailing moan.

Yet God the Father knows His children's needs,
   And should He chide, then say, "Thou knowest best,"
He paints the blossom, e'en the sparrow feeds,
   His trials lead to pure and perfect rest.

'Tis hard to bear the rod on quiv'ring flesh,
   And harder still upon the shrinking mind ;
But after rain the air is pure and fresh,
   And blinding snow preserves earth's fertile rind.

"OUT OF MUCH TRIBULATION."

The stormy wind strips bare the shivering trees,
   But purifies the air and makes it sweet;
And He who overrules all Nature, sees
   The joys and sorrows for His creatures meet.

And who are these who walk in robes of white,
   Who chant "Hosanna to the Heavenly King"?
The children, who in sorrow's darkest night
   Have seen the stars and heard their anthems ring.

Then courage, fainting soul! be not cast down,
   Sweep clean and garnish every secret place:
Though clouds are heavy and dark shadows frown,
   There is NO SHAME save MERITED disgrace.

Behold the great ones who in failure's hour
   Fulfilled the task which they were meant to do!
And never doubt that the Almighty Power
   Which worked for them, shall work as well for you.

THE MANY AND THE FEW.

SUNLIGHT was dancing through foliage green,
Glancing on herbage the tree trunks between;
Shadily resting we sat at our ease,
Speaking or silent, and fanned by the breeze;
Satisfied most of us with the faint gleam
Forcing its way like known facts through a dream.

Happily there in that twilight we lay,
Watching the birds and the insects at play;
No one seemed anxious to court the full beams
Which beat on th' meadow, and out on the streams
Glittered like burnished and dangerous steel,
Flashing from scabbards of horsemen who wheel.

Is it not so in the realm of the mind,
That the majority their pleasure find
Lazily loitering 'neath the deep shade,
Others opinions around them have made.
Which of us longs in the full rays of Truth,
Burthens to bear for the Truth's sake forsooth?

Fortunate 'tis that there are those who must
Leave all the comforts of shelter to thrust
Hands into wild nooks where specimens dwell,
Are not content in a deep shady dell
Idly away their brief life-time to pass,
Or be reflections displayed in a glass.

Restless and troublesome mortals are these,
Clearing the forests and searching the seas;
Always attaining, but never for long,
Singing in peace a glad victory song.
Rays of the truth cannot satisfy such,
Learning a little, they yearn to know much!

IN MAGDALEN CHAPEL.

(OXFORD, AUGUST 1890.)

A ROW of pictured saints obscures the light
    From rows of living faces in the stalls;
The glorious organ tones drown with their might
    The chorus of the birds outside the walls.

In this dim light, fresh faces of fair girls
    Look pale and faint, as those of sainted maids;
And as the rolling sound-storm circling whirls,
    The gloom increases and all colour fades.

The coarsest and least lovely countenance
    Grows spiritually delicate and wan;
And of frivolity's gay, wand'ring glance,
    All trace from the uplifted eyes is gone.

The upturned eyes catch the last pallid gleams
    Of day, and star-like, shine out wierdly clear,
Like corpse lights with their flick'ring, flashing beams,
    That dance o'er marshland when dread midnight's
        near.

Those many faces as 'fore God appear,
    As they shall be when time and storm are past,
When earth has faded, and the spirit near
    Its home, casts off the shrouding flesh at last.

God sees beneath the colour and the dress,
    Beneath the bloom of youth or gloom of age,
And on the soul he reads the true impress—
    Which men oft miss—writ on its hidden page.

FLEETING OR IMMORTAL.

I STOOD beside a garden gate that led
    Into the curving end of a short street,
And listened to the never-ceasing tread
    Upon a highway near, of many feet.

A sound of laughter surged as onward rolled,
    A restless tide of life no force may stem;
And as men passed, the solemn death-bell tolled,
    As though to ask, "What shall become of them?"

Are they but spray of Life's great ocean, tossed
    Against the beetling cliffs of transient time,
To shine a moment, then again be lost?
    To think so stung me sharply, like a crime.

Are they but blossoms on Life's spreading tree,
    Just born to bloom a moment in the sun,
Then fade away and die? Or shall they see
    Another life and light, when these are done?

They cannot die; of that I am quite sure,
    Though what their new life may be, who shall tell?
The spray falls back to ocean, blossoms pure
    Drop down to earth, nor stay just what they fell.

FLEETING OR IMMORTAL.

The sum of life, perchance, remains the same;
   In distribution only lies the change.
A form we knew by one familiar name,
   Transfigured, seems to us both new and strange.

If this be true of things we see and touch,
   We may believe it true of the unseen;
For laws that rule the little, guide the much,
   And nothing shall be lost that once has been!

OF BEAUTY.

O Beauty, glorious goddess, long defamed
   By foul Imagination's brooding fear,
   To which thy floating garments oft appear
The raiment of a temptress, boldly aimed
To win men from devotion that has tamed
   Unbridled passion in its wild career.
   To Wisdom's eyes wood-flowers are not more clear
Of taint than thou, and were as fairly blamed.

The world is steeped in Beauty to the lips,
   And only man avoids her winsome ways;
   He shuts his eyes to her diviner rays,
And at dark founts of bitterness he sips,
His nature's finest fibres rudely nips,
   To pass in gloomy twilight sunny days.
   A sparkling draught is proffered that allays
Life's thirst; through trembling hands the goblet slips!

Thy joyous presence, exquisitely fair,
   Transfigures with a touch the sordid lot,
   And life is little worth where thou art not.
Thy breath steals o'er the hills, and straight they wear
An undulating softness; thou dost fare
   To wreathe lithe tendrils round a sheltered spot,
   And soon th' enchanted and sequestered grot
Seems more than earthly to the lovers there.

With motions swift as beams of morning light,
   Thou playest across aspiring forest trees,
   Awaking answers to the rushing breeze
In flashes of reflected radiance bright,
Caught from the rising sun; then taking flight
   To ruffle the serenity of summer seas,
   Thou bringest to birth resounding harmonies,
Where wilful waves dash wildly, gem bedight.

All Nature yields with rapture to thy spell,
   And glad or sorrowful she owns thy sway;
   In narrow dales dost thou delighted stay,
Where far-extending uplands grandly swell,
And on those lofty peaks where few may dwell,
   So keen the air, so rare a balmy day;
   On level lands o'erlaid with misty grey,
Where mighty barriers the billows quell.

O Beauty, bring thy legions bright of joy,
   Flash rainbow tints of promise from thy wings
   On far serener eyes, where memory brings
Not scalding tears, but gentle rain; employ
These deadened senses till they cease to cloy
   The wheels of life, with gathered dust that clings
   To all neglected and untended things,
Corroding silently till they destroy.

My heart beats lightly as I think of thee,
    O Beauty, filling the unlovely haunts
    Of toiling men, where Ugliness now taunts
With bitter jibes of vice and poverty;
Transforming lanes to airy spaces, free
    From squalor; sad, distorted shape which flaunts
    Its rags so openly, and almost daunts
The hope of those who know what man should be.

O come, come quickly, fill the burthened breast
    With images of life instead of death;
    Revive the fainting soul till it draws breath
With mighty inspirations, making blest
Its days of labour and its hours of rest.
    Come like the Spring, that stirring softly, saith,
    "Awake" to every thing that quivereth
With life, to urge it on an upward quest.

Though puritanic forces long have fought
    A holy war against thee, come, renew
    Life's youthful joyousness once more; in lieu
Of hideous doubt, depression, narrow thought,
Bring open minds desiring to be taught
    How they shall pierce the darkness, and see through
    The Good and Beautiful, to find the True,
So long in man-made shadows vainly sought.

RE-UNION.

(SONG.)

I LONG to see thee once again,
    As thou wert years ago,
Ere the defacing hand of time
    Had forced thy tears to flow.

Thy soul is lovely as of old,
    'Tis but the fleeting face
That many years and grief untold
    Have wrapped in their embrace.

Death's portal passed, thou stand'st once more
    A maid serene and fair.
O linger near that crowded door,
    That I may join thee there.

CAST THY BREAD UPON THE WATERS.

Some words there are that float from age to age,
   Across the gulf of centuries thay fly,
Are ever fresh and black upon the page,
   Endued with life that knows not how to die.

Deep, elemental truths of love and life
   They bear upon their wings to thoughtful hearts;
They calm the passions, pouring oil on strife,
   Before their fragrance driven, doubt departs.

"Cast bread upon the waters," and believe
   The promise added to that strange command;
Assist the stumbling, false steps to retrieve,
   And lift the fallen with a gentle hand.

Not wealth nor honour do these duties bring,
   But inward riches rust can ne'er destroy;
A heart of sterling coinage and clear ring,
   Unmixed with worthless dross or dull alloy.

The seed, when sown, seems buried in the ground;
   But God works good in most mysterious ways,
And bread upon the water cast, is found
   Returning surely, after many days.

LYDIA.

WE sat, my friend and I, beside the fire,
   Within a quiet chamber. When she spoke
   It was as though my thought an echo woke.
"Does God," she asked, "the present day inspire?"

A silence fell between us after that,
   The waning daylight deepened into night,
   But on her face the flickering fire threw light;
While she as still as sculptured marble sat.

Her words went ringing through my wondering heart;
   Nor could I fail to note her wasted cheek.
   I waited quietly till she should speak,
The brooding thought more fully to impart.

A pause, and then, "If men were God-inspired,
   How did the inspiration seem to them?
   Was it an outward force they could not stem,
Or some internal impulse none admired?"

"Tell me," I said, "what prompts this question strange."
   "Since I have been so feeble," she replied,
   "Have thought, that as I am I might have died,
My mind has undergone a startling change;

"And day by day new thoughts grow clear to me ;
　　Of fixèd purpose I become aware,
　　The people whom I know seem now my care,
Though I before, forgot them utterly.

"And if I live I must go forth to find
　　The friendless and the fallen far or near ;
　　Must tell them of a Love which casts out fear,
Of God a Father, who loves all mankind.

"The life will be a hard one ; friends will chide,
　　And I, perchance, may doubt that I was right
　　To leave this home, so sheltered and so bright ;
While those who love me not, may e'en deride.

"Is this an inspiration? Am I mad?
　　What is this strange, new, pulsing life within,
　　This love for sinners, hatred for all sin,
This hot desire to make all sad lives glad?"

I dared not answer when she ceased to speak :
　　But soon remembered words began to flow,
　　" About my Father's business I must go,
The lost to find, the wand'ring sheep to seek.'

And then the answer came in one quick flash!
"God broods for ever o'er the changing world,
His thoughts in every age are lying furled;
'Tis He inspires the weak and makes them rash."

"I thank you." That was all she said, but now
A nurse goes fearlessly where strong men fear.
She tends the fallen, many sad ones hear
These words of life, "God loves e'en such as thou."

VARIETY.

WATCH thou the faces as they pass thee in the street,
    And see the beautiful, the coarse, the scarred with pain;
Some scowling back suspiciously, some very sweet;
    For two alike thou shalt look earnestly in vain!

Take then a bud or leaf from every plant and tree,
    And mark th' immense variety of shape and hue:
Again no two alike; the smallest is quite free
    To be its own true self, to drink from earth and dew.

Thy books are many, and 'twould be a childish thought
    Shouldst thou desire that all should tell the self-same tale.
Their value lies therein, that through them thou art brought
    To feel that minds are various, as are hill and dale.

For Multiplicity without satiety,
    All forms and colours tending ever to increase,
A universal law of life appears to be,
    The evolution of a force which cannot cease.

BEFORE THE CURTAIN.

Tinsel glitters on her gaze,
   Elfin forms and robes of light,
Filling her with glad amaze;
   O that life were half so bright!
Honied words of secret praise
   Draw her onward by their might,
Through illusion's golden haze,
   Fairy fountains pour delight.

Music wakes her slumbering heart,
   Stirring pulses still before,
Eager tremors wildly dart
   Through the senses' open door.
Hesitations all depart,
   Eagerly her thoughts implore
On a glittering race to start;
   Childlike joy can naught restore.

Falls the curtain, but her dream
   Hovers round her as she goes;
Flaring gaslights wildly gleam
   On the pavement, glamour glows
All around her, and they seem
   Flashing jewel fire that flows,
Widening to a glorious stream,
   Quenching all her girlish woes.

ON THE STAGE.

Future days shall be so fair,
    Every hour of purest gold,
Summer always in the air,
    Banishing dark nights and cold;
Silvery garments will she wear,
    Win great fame and wealth untold;
Sorrow shall not be her share,
    Clouds for her away be rolled.

. . . . . .

ON THE STAGE.

Rows of faces idly peer
    At her as her part she plays;
Gold itself were hateful here,
    And these tawdry tinsel rays
Flaunt before her, and appear
    Mocking spectres of past days.
Faces rising tier on tier,
    Haunt her on life's sodden ways.

Gone the glamour, beauty flies,
    Though so sorrowful, her part
Must be acted; sobbing cries,
    Stifled ere they leave her heart,
Dumbly ask the dearest prize,
    Liberty away to dart
From these unknown, curious eyes,
    Asking smiles, while tears will start.

Scented flow'rets, like a knife,
    Fall upon her tortured breast;
Martial music, drum and fife,
    Summon her to do her best,
Where forced gaiety is rife,
    Heedless of a soul oppressed.
Patience, weary one, the strife
    At its longest leads to rest.

Thundrous acclamations greet
    Th' idol of a giddy throng,
Roses raining at her feet
    Rapturously reward her song.
Nothing sees she but a street,
    And a girl who wends along
Picturing a life so sweet,
    Happy, innocent of wrong.

A FUSION OF MIND AND MATTER.

I sit with closèd eyes and listen long
To music militant, or plaintive song,
    And airy spaces rise,
        Where, 'neath o'erarching skies,
As far as sight can pierce, the mountains lift
Their rugged heads above the misty drift,

While murmuring streamlets fill
The valley warm and still,
With undertones of happy industry,
And prophecies of rivers yet to be.

Or, leaving men and cities far behind,
I climb into an eyrie where the wind
    Makes music ceaselessly,
    And roving eyes are free
To follow every undulating line,
And mark swift shadows fleet, and sunbeams
    shine;
    Melodious notes I know,
    With unknown accents flow,
To mingle in a symphony of space,
And bring a smile, or frown, on Nature's face.

Harmonious numbers and the breezy hills
Seem interfused within my breast; each fills
    The yearning heart with joy,
    And finds the soul employ,
Or, like sweet sleep, gives strength anew to wend
Upon the path where thought and action blend;
    Dissolving doubt to peace;
    And though the one should cease,
The other would bear witness through all time,
Of lofty heights the foot, or soul, may climb.

THROUGH BROTHER TO BROTHERHOOD.

In slavery and scorn
A Brother's love is born;
Egyptian bondage dark
Awakes th' heroic spark
Within the foundling's heart;
He takes his people's part,
Then leads them forth to go
Where milk and honey flow.
Through dangers manifold
To guide them; till grown old
He sees the Promised Land
Whereon he may not stand.

A fitful, flickering light
Shines through tradition's night;
It falls from men who pray
At morn and close of day,
" Jehovah, greatest Lord,
Keep Thou Thy pledgèd word,
And grant thy people peace
To grow and to increase."
Yet ruthlessly they smite
The weaker Canaanite!

BROTHERHOOD.

The veil is rent, and dying groans
Are echoed on earth's throbbing stones;
Upon a hill-top lifted high
A gentle Nazarene must die.
The Law to save its empire now
Binds thorns upon a tender brow;
The crucifix gleams luridly,
Yet failure's hour means victory!
On awe-struck hearts the last words fall,
And darkness covers with its pall
The place where Love departing, sighs,
Drain's earth's last cup, and fainting, dies!

"Forgive them, Father," accents new,
"Forgive, they know not what they do."
A wondrous sense of healing calm
Descends on men who came to harm;
Forgiveness sown within the breast
Shall germinate and know no rest;
Its precious seed is scattered wide
Upon the living, flowing tide
That bears to many lands the thought,
Self-sacrifice so nobly bought.
A banner everywhere unfurled
Proclaims, "The Father loves the world."

And soon the springing blades of wheat,
Preserved by cold and forced by heat,

Are clothing gloriously the fields.
Self-sacrifice a power wields
Beyond the might of crownèd king.
From land to land on buoyant wing,
Sweet messages of peace and joy
Awake each heart to full employ.
Too soon the plains are reaped once more,
Authority begins to store
In narrow walls the unripe grain;
With human blood the fruit they stain!

Dark clouds of strife and hatred hide the light,
Brother denounces brother; through the night
The Father, hidden by the smoke of creeds,
Seems careless of his crying children's needs;
And thousands groaning inly for pure food
Are forced to worship blocks of painted wood.
The lifted Cross of Love, become a scourge,
Is used to terrify and fiercely urge.
Yet nothing truly dies; burnt on a fire
Its emanations purified, inspire
With added heat the chill surrounding air,
And lo! there springs to life a blossom fair.

Ah see, where every persecuted maid,
And martyrs trapped, disfigured, and betrayed,
Translated, shine above the reek of strife,
And herald the return to quickened life

Of that great Sun no man hath power to stay;
Already the horizon gleams with day
When Law and Love to Freedom joined shall reign,
And hand shall meet with hand across the main;
When colour and condition, race and creed,
Shall be forgotten in a Brother's need;
When agony of one shall touch the whole,
And noble deeds shall pulse through every soul.

How long, how long, before the sunlight shall disperse
The mists, and rise above all fear of rough reverse?
Is consummation in the future yet afar,
And shall intolerance raise yet another bar
Between the men and nations, sharers of one Life,
That beats through every heart beneath the noise of strife?
Ah no! it cannot be, for God and man have met,
And soon the gloomy night of ignorance must set.
The golden days draw near, for thought is growing pure,
And loving hearts are waiting, ready to endure
With patience all the pangs of Brotherhood's late birth,
To bring the Paradise of Peace upon the earth.

"ONE THING I KNOW."

I KNOW not why I work to-day,
    Nor why I strive at this hard task;
I know not why I go to pray,
    And scarcely know what I would ask.

I know not what the end may be,
    And yet I toil as though I knew;
I know not why I would be free,
    Would suffer loss to be quite true.

Something there is that draws me on,
    And gives me strength to smile at pain;
Which pours out hope when joy is gone,
    And fills the empty heart again.

Something there is that bids me go
    Along a path I fear to tread;
It strikes the rock and waters flow,
    And touches stones to make them bread.

Yet ONE THING I most surely know,
    That this unseen, mysterious force
Evolves the higher from the low,
    Brings out the better from the worse!

PRESENT, THOUGH UNSEEN.

All day the rustling woodland,
  The whispering grass and flowers,
Beneath the summer sunshine
  Glowed green as fairy bowers.
But now the stars are shining,
  The earth is wrapped in shade,
I cannot see one flow'ret
  Within the gloomy glade.

The room is softly lighted
  By one lamp's pleasant glow,
And all around are standing
  The things I love and know.
But take away the glimmer
  Of that one cheery flame,
And all the rest are taken,
  I know them but by name.

Yet if the sun shone brightly
  By night as well as day,
The lamp were never lifted,
  Nor e'er consumed away;
I still should need my eyesight
  The greenwood's wealth to share;
Or recognise the treasures
  I know are standing there

To see the nearest object
    We need sight, light, and air ;
To touch it we need bodies,
    A solid garb 't must wear.
Yes, many things are present
    Which we can only guess,
We know them by their working,
    Or their resistlessness.

And who hath seen pure friendship,
    Though it is real and true?
Heat, motion, gravitation,
    These work unseen for you.
Then do not say things are not,
    That they can never be,
Remember the conditions
    Surrounding all you see!

A SUCCESSFUL MAN.

Not rich you say, and that is true,
   Nor hath he won great fame;
While his real worth is known to few,
   And some perhaps may blame.

He has not had an easy life,
   For he has told the truth,
And conscientiousness brings strife,
   Especially in youth.

But courage he has had and health,
   And ready, helpful hands:
The love of those he taught his wealth,
   Scattered in distant lands.

Many there are who owe to him
   Their love for nobler things;
At his name strong men's eyes grow dim,
   With tears that memory brings.

A SUCCESSFUL MAN.

    His houses have their walls of flesh,
        His lands are rescued minds,
    His gems are souls freed from the mesh
        Which pleasure round them winds.

    If such a man as this has failed,
        Then failure is success!
    The true success that has availed
        For other's happiness.

HOPE AND RESIGNATION.

Hope paints with sunset tints the leaden sky
Of long borne pain, of sorrow's coming night;
It shoots bright rays that whisper as they die,
The sun will come again with morning light.

Then work and hope if health should be thy portion,
Nor swerve from straightest paths of truth and right;
Defend the needy from unjust extortion,
And help the weak against the arm of might.

Endure and hope if weakness be thy part,
When flesh wears thin th' eternal world draws near.
God through His sick ones softens every heart,
The dew upon His harvest is a tear.

Be hopeful yet resigned, so shall thy days
Of active service, or of calm endurance,
Pass peacefully; that either of these ways
Leads home at last, is faith's sublime assurance.

TIMES OF TRANSITION.

ALL times are times of change, but youth and spring
   Are fullest of fresh life, and undismayed;
   Not long their eager footsteps are delayed
By solemn requiems they ought to sing;
And O, in days like these, when on the wing
   Are fancies manifold, and life is swayed
   By impulse from within, no boundary laid
Can measure what one year, e'en one, may bring.

A maiden quivers with delight to feel
   Strange streams flow in upon her narrow round,
   Exulting pulses dancing, leap and bound
In answer to importunate appeal
From the wide world without, whose echoes steal
   Upon her irresistibly, and sound
   On strings prepared to vibrate. Life is found
A growing wonder, and her senses reel.

Ascetic lives of still, monastic peace
   Are now impossible to living souls;
   Some force impalpable the mind controls,
And spirits, captive long, seek swift release,

And will not be denied ; the long, long lease
  Is over of imprisonment ; the poles
  Are scarcely far enough apart, and doles
Of freedom cannot bribe the strife to cease.

'Tis good to live in times of changing thought,
  When breezes freshly blow across the land,
  And many questions newly opened stand
Inviting eager minds abroad, to court
The glowing sunshine ; closèd doors long sought
  Monopolies to grant, to some small band,
  Of all-pervading light. New days demand
New watch-words, and new banners bravely wrought.

A stranger change than these awaits us all,
  And oft I wonder what that change shall be !
  Some are there, doubtless, who amazed shall see
Themselves as now they are, and wildly call
For sudden transformation. Death shall fall
  As falls a veil, O dying one, for thee ;
  The scene then changed, from flesh shalt thou be free,
But cherished hopes shall hold thee still in thrall.

For life is one ! In that room, or in this,
  The heart retains its many loves and hates ;
  An entered door stills not the wild debates
Of what I would not touch, or long to kiss.

Unhappy here and fretful, how shall bliss
   Miraculously fill, when pointing fates
   Have bid men try the other of two states,
Yet nothing, save the fleshly lusts, they miss?

Hold fast the thought, O soul, and live as thou
   Wert fain to live when, that transition made,
   Thou enterest the spirit-land arrayed
In that thou *thinkest!* Branded on the brow
By low desires, so well concealèd now
   That none suspect how far thy mind has strayed
   From virtue and from justice: how dismayed
Wert thou to-day, did *earth* no screen allow!

Some pass without a fear the narrow stream
   O'er which the mist of death its shadow flings;
   For them the tolling bell a joy-peal rings
Of hope lost in fruition; they but seem
As one awaking from a pleasant dream
   Of glorious sunshine, and unfailing springs,
   To find himself amid the beauteous things
Of which before, he caught a passing gleam!

THE ALTAR LAMP.

Leaving a busy, bustling street,
   We passed an unpretending door
Into a silent fane. Our feet
   Fell echoing on its massy floor.

Kneeling, we prayed; then through the gloom
   A far-off, faint, yet steady light
Shone star-like; by its ray the room
   Seemed vaster, solemn as the night.

That piercing light controlled the eye,
   Compelled the soul to own its power.
"Truth lives for aye," it seemed to cry,
   "Outlasts the creatures of an hour."

The organ pealed; some words were said,
   But through them all that shining spark
Burnt lonely. All the world seemed dead,—
   Truth, far away, illumed the dark.

"Ah, if these throbbing hearts bowed down
    Before the shrine could catch the flame,
And wander forth to hill and town,
    Proclaiming God's eternal Name.

"But no," I thought, "that light so pure,
    So far removed from those who pray,
Is guarded there; while men endure
    The toil and stress of every day.

"And yet 'tis well that Truth should burn
    Before an altar steadily,
That even two or three should turn
    From work to holy reverie.

"O were it not too far removed
    To fire the heart and rouse the brain!
It shines, a thing that may be loved,
    Not near enough for man to gain."

Harmonious tones disturbed my thought,
    A white-robed form moved o'er the floor;
And ah, from that far flame was brought
    A kindling spark for many more!

They shone more brightly than the first,
    Were nearer, yet were steady too;
To these e'en world-stained mortals durst
    Draw near, their fainting hearts t' renew.

In waiting souls they kindled fires,
   Transfiguring each careworn face
With chastened hopes and pure desires,
   With holy aspiration's grace.

Returning to the crowded street,
   Like consecrated ground it seemed;
On multitudes that onward fleet
   A new day dawned, a new sun beamed.

And every man and woman there
   Seemed nearer to the Heart Divine,
For each unconsciously doth bear
   A lamp to light at Truth's great shrine.

TRUE HAPPINESS.

They say thou'rt happy, that thy wit
    Lights up the dullest round of talk :
It may be so while lamps are lit,
    And men and women round thee walk.

A word for her, a smile for him,
    Thou listenest now with interest ;
But as I watch my eyes grow dim,—
    Thou art not what I once loved best.

Thy glance is piercing still, and bright,
    But not so earnest as of yore,
To seek and find what things are right;
    Thou jestest where thou didst adore.

Thou stately girl, nay, woman now,
    Throw off these shows that are not real ;
Return, and place upon thy brow
    The crown of thy youth's lost ideal.

Then could I truly call thee glad,
    Thou need'st not then dread quiet hours ;
No earthly loss could make thee sad,
    For sorrow would evolve new powers.

THE THIRST FOR KNOWLEDGE.

SHE tried to live as others live,
  To satisfy her mind as they,
To grasp the joy that love can give,
  To be content with childish play.

But all in vain! She could not rest,
  The garden walls seemed far too near;
Above the ivy's tossing crest
  Dream faces rose, to disappear.

"O let me see what lies beyond,"
  She cried, "though sight bring misery."
"Ah, go not hence," said voices fond,
  "Here surely thou hast liberty.

"Here dost thou reign despotic queen,
  And all is thine, for thou art loved;
Here thou art sheltered by the sheen
  Of silken curtains." Was she moved?

Yes, moved to go, and go full soon,
  Beyond that kingdom where she reigned,
To feel the scorching heat of noon,
  And know what others have attained.

To seek the sad and ask them why
    They suffer thus, yet cling to life;
To know the poor who live and die,
    Where endless toil and want are rife.

To share the heaven-born dreams oft sent
    Into the heart of fair, fresh youth;
And learn from men whose lives are spent
    In constant effort after truth.

'Tis some necessity that drives
    The sheltered from their Eden bowers:
" You must," the heart against it strives,
    And then " I will" is said 'mid showers.

Too oft alone the soul fares forth,—
    Always alone its choice must make;
Yet true as needle to the North,
    Its longing points the way to take.

A HARVEST VISION.

'Twas said, "How full of discontent to-day
   Are youthful lives; on restless feet they haste
   O'er foolish pleasures precious years to waste,
Though weary of the giddy games they play."

A vision rose of rustling fields all ripe,
   Awaiting willing workers to bring in
   A mighty harvest, stores of food to win,
Gaunt famine off the face of earth to wipe.

Of orchards glowing red with luscious fruit,
   Decaying on the branches, for no hand
   Is raised to gather it; of fertile land
O'errun with reptiles at its deepest root.

And then I saw a few untiring souls
   Who toiled the livelong day those fields to reap,
   With little time for rest or needed sleep,
Though far beyond their reach the upland rolls.

Ah, how shall two or three that giant task
   Accomplish? Manfully they strain and toil
   A few poor sheaves to save, lest all should spoil.
And O the shame that thousands idly bask!

I see them resting in the sheltered grove,
   Beside the stream, upon the breezy hill;
   Regardless of the harvest that should fill
The empty barns, they lightly sing and rove.

Their boisterous laughter drifts upon the air,
   Their heavy sighs oppress the leafy shades,
   And as they loiter, lo, their beauty fades,
While fretful fingers furrow lines of care.

So autumn days too swiftly slip away,
   Ungarnered grain is dropping to the ground,
   But while the sunshine lasts are idlers found
Who will not work, yet weary of their play.

At last come darkling days when all must rest,
   And many long that they could wholly die,
   So heavily a squandered past doth lie
On those who know they have not done their best.

The workers sleep ; yet sleeping, rouse new life,—
   Each earnest word and helpful deed awakes
   An echo in another heart, and takes
Perennial inspiration into strife.

HOME AGAIN!

I SEE her as she used to stand,
And shade her eyes with one brown hand
To gaze across the fields where lay
A line of smoke far, far away;
A power it wielded o'er her life,
For in her heart wild thoughts were rife.
She longed to try her maiden strength,
And to the town went forth at length.

I see her as she stood once more,
Outside that humble cottage door;
And ah, she fain would enter in,
But dared not go, because her sin
Had closed the door which once stood wide
In days when there was naught to hide;
When she and they who loved her well,
Had no sad tale of shame to tell.

The driving rain was falling fast,
And O, how bitter blew the blast
From those far hills that looked so fair,
When she, a girl, was standing there.

She wondered at her discontent,
And why into the world she went
'Mid strangers all alone to roam,
So far from that dear, sheltered home.

"O God," she wailed, "why was I born?"
And then her heart with anguish torn,
She sank with a despairing cry
Upon the doorstep wearily.
The aged mother heard the sound,
And reached the door with one quick bound;
Her face erst pale, grew darkly red,
She fell beside the lost one,—dead!

"THOUGHTS ARE THINGS."

On wings of thought the soul may soar above the sensuous, seen,
Beyond the realm of all that is, o'er shadows that have been,
To perch on lofty eyries, where afar extends the view,
Across the varied landscape of ideal worlds and true.

Though all life's glittering facets flash their tints upon his eyes,
Yet not the wisest man has seen where e'en his own life lies;
His Thoughts are Things by which he grasps the force he cannot see
To carve the shapeless future, till men know what she shall be.

And minds, creative by a power derived from God above,
Find thought the subtile atmosphere in which they live and move;
And every man may stand one day where prophets stood and taught,
Above the mists of sight and sense, where gleams of truth are caught.

"BENEATH THE STARS."

PACING beneath the stars
A sudden sense of the immensity
Of world-filled space went thrilling through me,
    And lo ! between the bars
Of light and shade around, I stood alone,
An atom of universe !   No moan
    Of anything so small
Could change that order so inviolate,
Or through infinitude reverberate,
    So faint, so faint its call.

    O'erwhelmed with solitude,
The cheerful flame of aspiration sank,
And penetrating mists rose cold and dank
    About me as I stood.
Oppressed with insignificance, I asked
Why aught so frail should be so sorely tasked,
    So restless to the core ;
" Unknown while living, and unmissed when dead,
Ah, what remains but to lay down the head
    In rest, and strive no more ? "

O heart, so sore dismayed,
All that magnificence has long endured,
And mortals weak as thou have felt assured
    That when they truly prayed
The Infinite hath harkened to their cry,
And hushed their terrors to serenity!
    The widest space is naught
    To omnipresent Thought,
Its wings omnipotent, and swift to bless,
    Flash down to earnestness.

    Soaring beyond thy strength,
Too anxious soul, thou'rt held in the embrace
Of dark despair, disabled for a race
    Of far, far shorter length.
Let palpitating pulses sink to rest,
Go, fill with joy some agonising breast,
    Soft harmonies shall rise
With cheerful answers to all questions sent,
Thy cup shall overflow with sweet content,
    And e'en the distant skies
    Seem nearer to thy eyes.

    E'en now I hear the feet
Of my own kind; they walk beneath the dome
Of spangled loveliness as in a home;
    Familiar voices greet

"BENEATH THE STARS."

These surging ears, recalling me to life,
To daily duties, and th' incessant strife
    Of good to conquer ill.
Almighty God, earth's sorrows now seem small,
The magnitude of space has dwarfed them all ;
    Subdue unto Thy will
    This heart serenely still.

THE GATE OF PEACE.

THROUGH a varied vale a throng
  All the sunny morning roamed ;
  Rippling laughter lightly foamed,
Breaking into flakes of song.

Drinking deeply at each fount,
  Resting under spreading shade,
  Ling'ring thoughtlessly they strayed,
Fleeting hours they failed to count.

Till the sun began to sink
  In the embers of the day,
  And the ghostly winding way
Forced them all to pause and think.

Darkness deepened all too fast,
  Like a thread the path rolled on,
  Every beam of day soon gone,
Dreary fear its fetters cast.

Anxious cries disturbed the air,
  Heavy groans aroused the night,
  Putting peace and joy to flight,
Throwing loads of carking care.

THE GATE OF PEACE.

Till a silent watcher spied
   Portal narrow, grim, and dark,
   Lighted by one flickering spark.
Thitherward the wanderers hied.

Knocking timidly one asks
   Shelter from the drenching dew;
   "Welcome, welcome, those of you
Willing to attempt our tasks.

"Narrow is the gate, and ease
   All unknown to those who pass;
   Close behind it dense clouds mass,
Deep the river, keen the breeze.

"Yet, O mortals, do not fear,
   Step by step on solid ground
   Are the faithful footsteps found;
Slough and whirlpool are not here.

"One step taken clears the road
   For a bolder step to come;
   Though your songs be frozen, dumb,
Wild despair shall cease to goad.

"Though your happy laughter cease,
   Marching music, solemn, slow,
   Cheers courageous souls that go
Through their Duty into Peace."

TWIN-STARS.

Beneath laburnam's dappled shade
   She sat with face down-bent,
While summer breezes round her strayed
   And kissed her as they went.

The olive pallor of her face,
   Voluptuously sweet,
In northern lands seemed out of place,
   For sun and passion meet.

Down-drooping lids concealed her eyes,
   I guessed them dark and deep;
Impatient as each moment flies
   Their hidden charm to reap.

Uprose a lark with merry shout
   And roused her from her trance;
Then looking up, she gazed full out
   With keen, observant glance.

And lo! the eyes were clear and blue,
   A goodly space apart,
Fair lakes of purity, and few
   Lay bare to such the heart.

TWIN-STARS.

Those eyes met mine as strangers' meet,
   With questioning in their gaze;
I longed to linger at her feet
   That she my life might raise.

And though we never met again,
   Those eyes aroused my soul;
They haunted me when life seemed vain
   And lifted high its goal.

In quiet hours I see them still,
   So steadfast and so sweet,
Twin-stars subduing to their will
   The heart they came to greet.

THE PURSUIT OF PLEASURE.

A FLOATING nymph, in gossamer arrayed,
    Came o'er the meadow to a garden fair ;
Before a rose-crowned arbour paused, and stayed
    To watch a brooding youth reclining there.

His curling hair in wild confusion lay
    Around a face a goddess well might love :
He heeded not the glorious summer day.
    "I'll tempt him," so she thought, "with me to rove."

A gentle laugh, like chiming of a flower,
    Fell on his idle senses, and he smiled ;
She laughed again ; he gazed around the bower
    With startled attitude, and glances wild.

Then looking through the porch around the door
    He saw a shape, diaphanous and sweet :
She raised her filmy veil as to explore
    The dusky chamber, that their eyes might meet.

She smiled and beckoned with bewitching grace,
    The youth looked long at her and found her fair ;
Then one step forward moved he from his place.
    A cold, yet gentle hand detained him there !

He turned, amazed to learn what this might be!
　　The arbour had but now seemed empty quite;
And yet *one* held him, *one* hung gracefully
　　Almost within his reach, and bathed in light!

A shadowy form it was, in dusky grey,
　　That seemed to keep him firmly where he stood.
His inmost soul was urging him to stay,
　　But she, outside, put on a sportive mood.

She feigned to go, then turned again to him,
　　Unveiled her golden head which glittered, flashed!
Soft words she whispered; all the world grew dim,
　　And forward to lay hold of her he dashed.

She fluttered hither, thither, sometimes near,
　　Sometimes so far away that he despaired;
But when his ardour waned, she would appear
　　To wait for him, as though for him she cared.

Upon the waves of growing passion tossed
　　He noticed not that she grew coy and cold:
His home, his friends, his honour, all were lost
　　To follow her o'er plain, and sea, and wold.

His youth and beauty waned; unhonoured age
　　Crept over his disfigured, wrinkled brow.
He ran till he could run no more, then rage
　　Awoke, and fierce revenge he 'gan to vow.

THE PURSUIT OF PLEASURE. 259

"O Traitress," so he groaned, "for whom my life
    Was wasted, I could kill thee, even thee."
"Nay, nay," she answered," thou gav'st up all strife ;
    Saw'st thou not Wisdom that day, holding thee ? "

"But she was dull," he cried, "and cold, and still ;
    How could I know that *she* was pure and good ? "
"Frail man," said Pleasure, "hadst thou had the will,
    She had become an angel where she stood !

"We two are sisters, she and I ; and she
    Brings me to those who choose her quiet road :
But they who leave all else to follow me,
    Find ashes on their lips, and me their goad ! "

He looked, and lo ! her airy shape had changed
    Into a loathsome hag, lean, lank, and grim ;
And all her foolish children round her ranged,
    To join their brotherhood invited him.

A moment he despaired ; " Is this the end
    Of all I hoped in boyhood and in youth ?
Must I with this sad band for ever wend,
    And carry in my heart Despair's fierce tooth ? "

With shuddering repugnance he turned round,
    "If I must die, I'll die alone," he said.
In Wisdom's hand his burning hand he found,
    And she his trembling footsteps gently led.

She laid him softly on the short, sweet grass.
 "I cannot teach thee much, O weary soul;
Thy wasted years unfit thee here, alas,
 To comprehend thy life's divinest goal.

"But thou hast even now begun the strife,
 Of the immortal o'er the mortal part;
Move on without a fear, the future life
 Shall grant thee chances to make clean thy heart."

www.ingramcontent.com/pod-product-compliance
Lightning Source LLC
Chambersburg PA
CBHW031959230426
43672CB00010B/2210